MINDFULNESS FOR KIDS

Mindful Techniques for Managing Emotions, Overcoming Anxiety, and Boosting Confidence for a Happier, Calmer Life

Abby Swift

Copyright © 2024 Abby Swift

Published by: Bemberton Ltd

All rights reserved. No part of this book or any portion thereof may be reproduced in any form, by any electronic or mechanical means, without permission in writing from the publisher, except for the use of brief quotes in a book review.

The publisher accepts no legal responsibility for any action taken by the reader, including but not limited to financial losses or damages, both directly or indirectly incurred as a result of the content in this book.

ISBN: 978-1-915833-45-7

Disclaimer: The information in this book is general and designed to be for information only. While every effort has been made to ensure it is wholly accurate and complete, it is for general information only. It is not intended, nor should it be taken as professional advice. The author gives no warranties or undertakings whatsoever concerning the content. For matters of a medical nature, the reader should consult a doctor or other health care professional for specific health-related advice. The reader accepts that the author is not responsible for any action, including but not limited to losses both directly or indirectly incurred by the reader as a result of the content in this book.

View all our books at **bemberton.com.**

TABLE OF CONTENTS

5	**Introduction**
13	A Simple Introduction to Mindfulness
31	What Is Our Mind, Anyway?
45	The Basic Mindfulness Technique
63	Insight: Why Mindfulness Works
77	Different Ways to Apply Mindfulness in Everyday Life
87	Riding the Wave of Emotions: Feelings, Anger, Anxiety, and Stress
101	What to Do When Difficult Feelings Show Up
113	Mindfully Coping with Stress
123	The Real "Me" Versus My Ideas About Me
135	Navigating Life's Big Changes
147	Practical Mindfulness to Guide a Happy Life
169	**Conclusion**

INTRODUCTION

"Today you are you! That is truer than true!
There is no one alive who is you-er than you!"
"I'm afraid that sometimes you'll play lonely games too.
Games you can't win 'cause you'll play against you."
— **Dr. Seuss**

Did you know that, throughout your whole life, there is one person who can help you the most, love you the most, and teach you the most? That same person may also be the one who can hurt you the most. Can you guess who that person is? (If you haven't guessed already, there's a clue in the poem from Dr. Seuss above.)

That's right — it's you.

Even your own parents and your very best friends can't always help you as much as you can help yourself. And in the same way, not one of them — not your teacher, your mom or dad, your bestie, or even that bully at school — can annoy, bother, undermine, or hurt you as deeply as you can your very own self.

Why is that? It's because, of all the people in this whole world, the one who gets to know you best is *you*. The one who really knows all your deepest secrets and all your innermost thoughts and feelings is you.

You're the one who gets to think what you think and feel what you feel. No other person can live your life for you, and nobody knows exactly, precisely, and in perfect detail what it's like to be you. Only you know that. Only you get to fully experience that. You're the one who gets to decide, in the end, what you like or don't like. In your own heart, you decide who or what you love, what you really believe, and who you are.

Being Your Own Best Friend

None of us will go through our entire lives alone. We get to have relationships with all kinds of people. We have parents, and maybe we have brothers or sisters. We probably have friends, and we might also have enemies — or, in rare cases, even arch enemies! But of all the many different kinds of relationships, the most important — and the most interesting of all — is the relationship we cultivate with ourselves.

This book is all about that relationship — and, in an important way, that's what mindfulness is all about.

Mindfulness is something that goes right to the heart of you. It teaches you how you can best love yourself, and that's why it's so interesting and useful.

"What is mindfulness?" you might ask. Well, the best way to explain it is to show you directly.

How to Be Mindful

Try this. When you get to the next " * " in the middle of the page, close your eyes for a moment. Try to notice the very next thought that comes into your head. Try really hard to see where that thought comes from, and where it goes.

*

Now, in the same way, try to sense the very next feeling that comes to you. Where do you feel that feeling?

*

Whatever you thought or felt is just what it is. Don't worry about it at all — that's not really the point right now. Maybe you didn't think anything at all, and maybe you can't even explain what you felt. Whatever it was, that's fine. The point of the exercise is just to pay attention. The whole point is to look inwards, into your very own self.

What you have just done, while you were noticing or becoming aware of your own thoughts and feelings, is called "mindfulness."

That word is actually strange, in a way, because when we try to do it, we feel our minds go a bit empty, rather than full. And that's really the point! Don't worry if that sounds confusing, we'll explain all of this as we go along.

You could say that mindfulness is almost like an art — it's the art of being able to be the best you possible. It's the art of really being aware of who you are, deep down — and being perfectly happy with that, just as it is. It might sound really simple, but when we try to do it, it's not always that easy.

That Voice in Your Head

Have you ever found yourself having an "imaginary conversation" in your head? Do you have conversations quietly inside yourself, without speaking a word? Now here's an interesting question: Who was talking to whom?

You were talking to yourself, right? There aren't two different people in there, after all!

Talking to ourselves is a way for us to sort out our thoughts and feelings, and it's sometimes called "self-speak."

It's a useful practice and a handy tool that we human beings use all the time. But it's also a bit of a curse.

We can use self-speak to figure all kinds of things out, especially when there's nobody smarter around to talk to. But it can also create a problem, because self-speak can sometimes turn into self-bullying. That's when our relationship with ourselves starts to become unhealthy. Interestingly, we're usually not even aware that it's happening — and that's the opposite of mindfulness.

Basically, mindfulness means becoming more aware of what we are telling ourselves in our heads. It helps us to have healthy, positive self-speak. We're going to explore how to do that in this book.

These are just a few of the most important ways that becoming more mindful can help us. It's especially useful when we are feeling anxious or nervous. It helps us to learn how to trust ourselves in a deep way, and how to trust life, too. It also helps us remember love, even when things seem awful.

Does that sound like something you would like to master? If so, this book is going to show you how to start this important journey. In the end, it's up to you to make it work for you in your own life, but you will find all the tools you need to get you started here in these pages.

How Does Mindfulness Help Us?

- It makes us far more self-aware, in a good way.

- It helps to focus our minds, making us a bit smarter as a side-effect — and much wiser too.

- It is a wonderful tool for dealing with anxiety, stress, panic attacks, and fear.

- It helps us better deal with change.

- It helps us to have compassion — we feel more empathy and love for ourselves and other people.

- It helps us to better handle bad moods, difficult emotions, and difficult situations in life.

- It helps us accept ourselves just as we are, no matter how that is.

- It also helps our bodies, minds, and emotions to remain healthy.

1

A SIMPLE INTRODUCTION TO MINDFULNESS

So, What Is Mindfulness?

Mindfulness is all about paying attention to the present moment—and doing so on purpose. It means paying attention in a very special way. It goes much deeper than merely saying, "I'm paying attention," and then skipping on to the next thought. It means becoming absorbed in the real, living, present moment.

It's not about yesterday, and it has absolutely nothing to do with tomorrow. It's all about how we consciously and deliberately decide to show up for real life *here* and *now*.

The secret is this: If you're not mindful, you don't get to consciously decide how you show up. Instead, you will show up and engage with your life on something like "autopilot mode." It will be as if some important part of you is asleep. (We can call that sleeping part of us our deeper awareness.)

If your "default mode" of being you is scared, angry, jealous, or upset, then that's how you might go through your whole life—and that might not be much fun.

If your default mode of showing up for life is what you actually want—in other words, happy—then that's what you will tend to get instead (at least more often than not).

It's your choice, of course.

Why? Because nobody else can make you happy on your behalf. Other people might do things that trigger unhappiness in you, but nobody can keep mulling over bad feelings on your behalf. Only *you* get to decide what to hold onto in your mind and heart. Mindfulness helps us remember that important fact.

Mindfulness gives us a moment of awareness in which we get to decide.

For instance:

"I feel a little sad today, and I wish that were different. But I'm here. I'm alive. I'm not going to avoid life today. I'm awake and switched on. I choose to accept things as they are. I choose to be kind to myself, and to other people and other things, too. I choose to forgive myself, to love myself, and to support myself — and all the other people and things that I can, too."

Your own voice might sound a little different, but that's the basic idea.

If you're not mindful, the sad thoughts will just grab ahold of your mind and spoil your whole day, often without you even being aware that it's happening.

How Does It Work?

When a difficult emotion, like sadness, fear, or anger, comes around the corner and confronts us, mindfulness helps us to change things around. We get to choose what this difficult feeling means to *us*.

It's still hard to deal with the bad feeling. Mindfulness isn't like a magic pill—but it is like a lifeline. It connects us and brings us back to the present moment, instead of being lost in an ocean of emotions and thoughts for too long.

The key is to pay attention and create some space around your own thoughts and feelings.

So, it's just paying attention?

Sometimes a teacher or our parents might remind us with a sharp voice, "Pay attention!"

That's because they want us to focus on something important. Mindfulness is a little different. It's not so much about paying attention to a lesson, an instruction, a specific person, a word, or a thing. It's more about remembering to be present.

That means paying attention to the here and now—all of it, including ourselves. It also means taking judgment out of our attention. Instead, it means bringing a kind, nurturing feeling into our attention. The attention we pay becomes as pure and clean as water.

The idea is to pay attention to whatever is really going on right now, and to know that you are here, paying attention. It's like checking in with yourself: "I'm here. Present!"

Mindfulness switches on our natural human sense of curiosity and our sense of wonder. It opens the door to knowing all kinds of wonderful things. Most importantly, it helps you to know *you*.

How Does That Help?

Far too often, we're off in our heads somewhere. We're thinking about what happened yesterday, or what might happen tomorrow. We're thinking about what we'd rather be doing. We're thinking about what we like, and what we don't like. We're sitting up in our heads, judging the present moment as good, bad, or boring. We're thinking about what might go wrong, and how that might feel.

We might even beat ourselves up with those conversations in our head. We might start believing hurtful and harmful things about ourselves, because we keep telling those things to ourselves, over and over. That's called "negative self-speak."

Mindfulness brings us back. It grounds us in ourselves, almost as if we're coming back into our own skin again. It's like rebooting the live computer inside us, and resetting it to "natural."

"Wait a minute! I'm actually alive and present. Before I think or feel anything at all, life is actually happening right now."

Life is so mysterious, and there's always something interesting happening. We just need to have the eyes to see it. Mindfulness helps us reclaim that superpower.

We start to notice things. Sometimes they are just little things: "Here's my hand. How weird is it to have a hand? This is how the skin on my hand feels. I'm alive, and this is what it feels like to be alive. Nice!"

We notice the little details of life that we tend to take for granted, like the beauty of the sky, the weirdness of bugs and plants, or the way shadows move on the walls. We start noticing smiles and good things that are happening. We're not so terribly upset when bad things happen.

Now there's time and space to actually appreciate and savor those things, instead of rushing off to the next thing (and the next, and the next, etc.). Instead of killing time with video games, Internet scrolling, or idle chit chat, we actually start *living*.

Too often, we rush around wanting to do lots of things because our minds are restless. Mindfulness calms our minds, recharges our energy, and grounds us in the present moment. It inspires us to "walk as if you are kissing the Earth with your feet" (that's a quote from the Buddhist teacher Thich Nhat Hanh).

A Quick Look Back: Where Did Mindfulness Come From?

Mindfulness is a very old life hack. In fact, it's ancient. You could say that it has been around for almost as long as people have been thinking.

It didn't take humans long to figure out that thinking is both a blessing and a curse. Brain power might help us survive better, but it also comes with a downside: overthinking things and worrying too much about every little detail.

Somebody wise came up with a great antidote: mindfulness.

Nobody really knows who that wise person was, but we do have a few clues that show us that it was an idea that worked. So, people started teaching other people about it. Luckily, a few of them kept on teaching, and the method has been passed down to us, more or less intact. It looks a little different today, but the basic idea is the same.

If we go back in history, to a time before people bothered to write things down — almost 5000 years ago! — we find a kind of mindfulness. Join me in your imagination, and let's take a look.

Ancient Times

Imagine that we're going back through the mists of time and skipping across the globe to the land of India. We're zooming in, down into a hot, green jungle. We're going in between the trees, where we can hear the jungle sounds and smell the moist air.

When we reach the ground, there is a simple hut made out of sticks, leaves, and mud. In front of the hut sits a very strange man.

He has a long beard, and he looks old, but his face appears young and clear. His eyes are half open and half closed, and he's sitting with his legs crossed.

He's not doing anything. In fact, he's sitting so still that he looks almost like a statue. He's known in this area as a great guru, or teacher. Do you know what he's doing? Let's ask him!

"Excuse me, sir, we don't mean to interrupt, but would you mind telling us what you're doing?"

After a moment, the man seems to come back from very far away and notice us. There is a look of complete calm and deep serenity on his face. He smiles, and says, "It is called meditation. That means I wasn't doing anything at all!" He chuckles.

"What were you thinking about?"

The man smiles mysteriously. After a while, he answers, "It is not what I was thinking about that is important. It is not a *thought* that I was exploring. It is that which does the thinking; that by means of which thought is possible." He chuckles again.

"I am aware of my awareness. I am that." He smiles again in the most mysterious way, so peacefully, as if he doesn't have a care in the world — like a happy kid. Then he goes back to meditating, as if we're not even here.

Meditation is like an advanced kind of mindfulness. The practice of meditation and mindfulness spread across the world a long time ago. Not everyone knew about it, but it was there. You might say the idea lived a kind of underground life. It was taught by wise masters, like our strange guru.

Join me now in your imagination again. We're leaving the hot jungles of India and flying through time and space. We're skipping forward a few centuries and heading over to the island nation of Japan, during the time of Zen.

The Time of Zen

Deep in the mountains, shrouded in mist, there is an old monastery. It is far away from the hustle and bustle of city life. A group of happy Zen monks are practicing the art of Zen archery. The teacher is a wise old sensei, and he has told them the secret. "Don't think, and don't worry," he reminds them.

The young monks are trying very hard to do that, but most of them are not able to. The sensei encourages them.

"When the arrow goes exactly where you know it will go, then you are in a state of flow. You have become one with the arrow, and one with yourself. If you think about it, if your mind is somewhere else, or, worse, if you worry about it, then you will fail."

He demonstrates. One of the junior monks blindfolds him, and, even though the sensei can't see the target, he fires an arrow.

It goes straight into the bullseye.

None of the others are ready to try that. Their minds are not yet peaceful enough — but practice makes perfect.

During most days, the Zen monks lead a quiet and simple life. When they are not fetching water or sweeping floors, they're tending the gardens and growing food. Most evenings, they attend lessons, and then they meditate.

Tonight's lesson is meant to help a young monk who struggles with anxiety.

The sensei tells them a little story: "A few years ago, there was an anxious monk here. We called him Ito. One night, everyone woke up to a big noise. Ito was yelling at the top of his voice.

"I almost stepped on a venomous snake, and it nearly killed me!" He was yelling, and then he told the others to bring medicine, just in case. Everyone woke up, and rushed to see and help. When the other monks brought more light, do you know what they found? There, coiled up in the corridor — was a harmless piece of rope."

Some of the monks can barely contain their laughter. The sensei looks around the room and raises an eyebrow.

"Does anyone know what this story means?"

"Ito was an idiot!" shouts one of the braver monks. With that, everyone begins to laugh.

"That may be so," replies the sensei calmly, "although Ito was actually a very clever man. But his mind was restless. Because his mind was not at peace, he saw danger where there was no real danger. He constantly saw trouble where there was no trouble."

The sensei pauses for a moment and strokes his long, silver beard.

"A restless mind is trouble. Mindfulness is the antidote!"

When our minds are calm, we won't imagine all kinds of trouble where no trouble exists. That's one of the most important insights from the time of Zen.

The ancient wisdom of mindfulness weaved its way through people's lives in many places and times, and somehow, it found its way to our time, too. Let's follow those threads through time and space and see where they lead.

More Modern Times

The swirling vortex of our space-time portal clears.

It's 1979, and we've landed in the United States. We're somewhere inside the Massachusetts Medical School. In fact, we've landed down in the basement (and no, that's not due to a miscalculation!).

Down here in a big room that isn't being used, a man called Jon Kabat-Zinn is teaching a new kind of class, never before seen in Western schools. It's called "Mindfulness-Based Stress Reduction," or MBSR for short. A small group of people are learning the basic techniques of mindfulness.

Jon is helping them deal with stress, anxiety, depression, pain, and worry. His students include all kinds of people who have struggled with different things in life. Some are depressed, some are recovering from an illness, and some are victims of trauma. Others are what you might call plain old nervous Nellies — they just worry a lot.

He is teaching them all how to become aware of their own thoughts and feelings.

"Don't judge your thoughts and feelings as good or bad," he reminds them. "Make space around them, and pay attention to that space in which the thoughts and feelings appear." He teaches them breathing techniques and mindful ways to engage with life.

After the class, many of his students feel a sense of peace. They start telling others about their experiences. Little by little, the word "mindfulness" starts to get around.

Jon was inspired to teach this class when he learned about Zen, while he was still a student. He decided that it was such good medicine that he would dedicate his life to teaching people all about mindfulness. But he also wanted to combine it with the benefits of modern Western science.

Today, mindfulness has become an idea that many people know about—and that's thanks to people like Jon.

Why Mindfulness Is Super Useful for You, Right Now

If you struggle with anxiety, pain, difficult emotions, or frequent sadness, this is great medicine for your mind and heart. If you often feel restless or bored, then mindfulness is good for you, too. Even if you're basically happy most of the time, it can still improve your life in subtle ways.

Mindfulness helps us with whatever we are doing. We could be eating, playing a game, learning something, or just walking, and mindfulness will add something special to the experience.

It makes us feel "more here." It makes us feel natural. Or, to put it another way, it restores our "muchness."

What you have to do is pay more attention, in a very special way. In return for "paying attention," you get:

- A deep sense of mental and emotional openness.
- Stress-free spontaneity.
- Balance and calmness.

- You get to feel more alive, more healthy, and more switched on.

- Life seems a lot more interesting, even in those boring or awful moments.

When we're mindful, it feels like there's more time and more room in which to enjoy life. We create a comfortable, open space for ourselves, all around us.

That peaceful, accepting "vibe" that shines from inside us gets noticed by other people, and they respond well.

We create that "space" in our heads and our hearts, and we show up for life from that comfortable, natural place.

Are you interested to find out more about how and why mindfulness works? First, we need to learn a few things about our minds and our brains. In the next chapter, we will explore how all of that works.

WHAT IS OUR MIND, ANYWAY?

Our brains and our minds are wonderful, complicated, mysterious things. Even though scientists have studied them, poked them, prodded them, and pondered over them for a long time, there are still many important questions that remain unanswered.

Are you aware that your mind and your brain are not the same thing?

- Your **brain** is a physical organ in your body. It's the spongy gray mass of cells between your ears. There are about 80 to 100 **billion** brain cells in there!

- Your **mind** is even more complicated. It's not a physical thing that you can hold. It's a complex network of ideas, pictures, words, associations, beliefs, memories, filters, and so much more besides that!

Here are interesting questions for a wise young person:

Who (or what) is it that looks out from behind your two eyes? Who or what is aware of the thoughts in your head, and the feelings you have? What is it that can become aware of both the brain and the mind?

These are deep questions, and the truth is, there are many different types of answers. You might enjoy exploring them in detail one day, if you're a deep thinker.

The simplest, most straightforward answer one might give is this: "It's me. I am *self-aware*."

Of course, that begs the next question: Who or what am I, really? That's something you might want to wrestle with someday, too — it's up to you! But beware, philosophers have been trying to answer that one for centuries!

Even though the mind is shrouded in a bit of mystery, we do know quite a lot about our brains. We also know at least some of the basic ways in which our minds work. This can be useful information if we want to get to know ourselves better.

Discovering How Our Brains Work!

Our brains control what goes on in our bodies. They are like the boss of all the other organs.

Our brains manage our breathing, our heartbeat, the blinking of our eyes, and the way we use our five senses — all of this and quite a lot more, besides. Millions of messages travel between our brains and our bodies via electrical impulses and chemicals. It happens lightning fast, and all the time.

Because it's so important for life, our brain is protected by a thick membrane and a fairly thick, bony skull. Even so, it's wise to wear a helmet whenever you do something potentially dangerous (or stupid!).

The brain has different regions that take care of different things. Here are some of the most important ones:

1. **Amygdala**. This is an almond-shaped structure on either side of the brain. It is likely quite active during your current phase of life. It continues to develop late into our teenage years and is what most affects our emotions. Right now, it controls much of your experience of life, and that's why you may struggle with emotions quite often. Later, it will get a little easier.

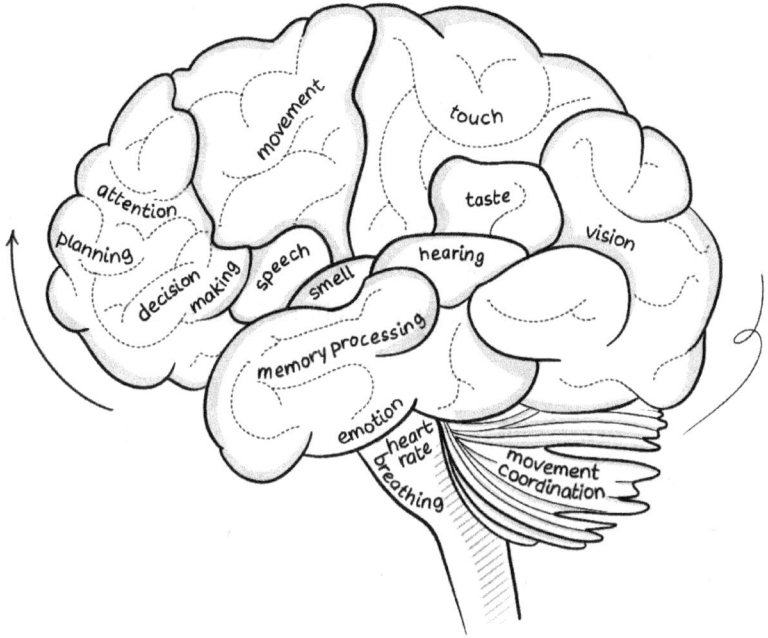

2. **Cerebellum**. You'll need a well-developed cerebellum if you want to ride a skateboard, dance, walk gracefully, or even stand up straight. The cerebellum is located at the back of the brain, and it's fairly small compared to the cerebrum. It mostly controls our body movements.

3. **Brain stem**. As the name suggests, this is located at the stem of the brain, where the brain joins the spine. This part of our brain controls our involuntary actions. These include our heartbeat, our digestion, and so on — the things that take care of themselves without us having to think about it.

When your heart races and you start to sweat because you've been active, that's your brain stem at work, sending signals and making sure your body gets what it needs at the right time.

4. **Pituitary gland**. This pea-sized gland in your brain has an important job. Among other things, it influences the way your whole body grows and develops. When we reach puberty and go through all those hormonal changes, the pituitary gland is working overtime.

5. **Pineal gland**: This is another very important gland that sits in the middle of the brain. Weirdly enough, the pineal gland contains a few light-sensitive cells, similar to the ones in your eyes. One of its jobs is to regulate your sleep cycle. Also — and this is important for our theme — scientists now suspect that mindfulness specifically helps this gland work better. In turn, that helps you sleep better when you're supposed to sleep, and wake up when you're supposed to be awake.

6. **Cerebrum**. This is the biggest part of the brain. It's what helps you move all your voluntary muscles (like in your arms and legs) and think about things (like math problems). It has two halves. Scientists think that the right half allows us to think abstract thoughts, like composing music. The left half is more logical. It helps us build things and figure out logical problems.

7. **Prefrontal cortex**. This is the front and topmost part of our brain, and it's the one that develops last. Right now, it's likely still developing in you. By the time we're more or less adults, at around age 25, it reaches basic maturity. But our brains keep on changing and developing as we continually learn new things. The prefrontal cortex helps us with higher reasoning, developing wisdom, and thinking about complicated things. It's also where we do most of our worrying, by the way!

That's quite a lot of information to digest. Luckily, we don't need to memorize it all in order to master mindfulness.

These are just some of the basic things that our brains do for us. It helps us understand what's going on when we think about things and feel emotions.

As we are growing up, our brains and our bodies are developing in lots of interesting ways. There's a whole lot happening inside of us. Sometimes, the changes are unexpected and awkward. It takes time to learn new skills and cope with new thoughts and feelings.

Sometimes, we might feel a bit overwhelmed. If that happens to you, please take courage — you're not the first human being to go through these things. Most of us turn out okay!

Mindfulness can help us navigate some of these difficult changes more smoothly. So now, let's put this information into context.

Connecting Dots: How Our Thoughts, Feelings, and Actions Are All Linked

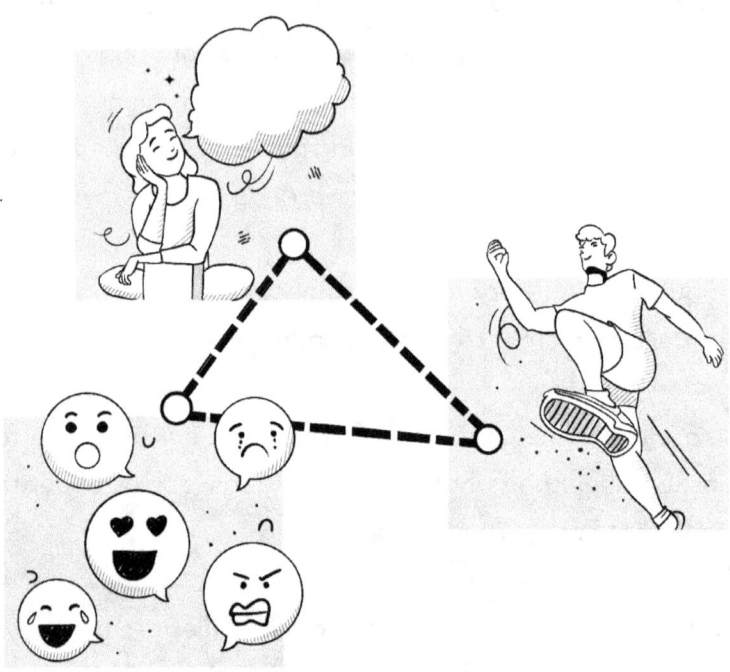

Imagine being driven to school in an old-fashioned, horse-drawn carriage, with a driver wearing a top hat! It might sound funny, but this is actually a useful illustration. It shows the way our bodies, feelings, and minds work together. Allow me to explain.

Our body is a bit like that carriage. It's the physical vehicle that gets us through our journey of life. Our emotions are somewhat like the horses that pull the carriage. They're what give us the energy—

the drive — to get up and go. Our rational minds are like the driver that holds the reins in his hands. The mind decides which route to take.

What we call our sense of self — the feeling of being "me" — is like the passenger sitting in that carriage.

All these different parts of us work together as a whole. Through mindfulness, we help to make sure that each part is doing what it is supposed to do.

When we know ourselves better, then we can understand ourselves better. That way, we can get along well with ourselves — we can get to the destination we want to go to, and it's a smoother ride.

Journeying Through Life in Our Carriage

As we go through life, we have lots of different kinds of experiences. Some belong to the carriage, some to the horses, and some to the driver — in other words, our body, emotions, and mind.

Here's an example. Besides what we sense with our eyes, ears and noses, we also feel things in our bodies. We might feel hungry, or sleepy, or full of energy.

We also feel what we call emotions — like sadness, fear, anger, joy, and other feelings.

Our body feelings and emotional feelings are linked together the way the horses are tied to the carriage with leather straps and poles.

Sometimes, it's hard to say where the body feelings end and the emotions begin — like when we're angry, for instance. Our "blood boils," so to speak. We feel something like heat and tension in our bodies, but there's an angry emotion, too.

Our emotions affect our bodies, and our bodies influence our emotions. Healthy minds and healthy emotions go along with healthy bodies.

Just like those powerful horses pulling a carriage, our emotions sometimes have a mind of their own. It's hard to predict how we are going to feel, and it's hard to control those feelings sometimes. When horses panic, they might bolt and drag the carriage along, causing damage. It's the same with our emotions. If they get out of hand, it can be dangerous. We need them, though, because without them, life would be quite empty. We'd have no drive and no motivation to do things.

Our minds are also linked to our feelings and our bodies, the way the carriage driver sits and holds the reins. A good carriage driver knows exactly how to work with his horses. In the same way, a mindful person knows how to think about their feelings, and how to direct their emotional energy. This is a great skill and one worth learning in life.

WHEN THE RIDE ISN'T SO SMOOTH

Sometimes, the different parts of us seem to want different things. For example, our body wants to sleep in for another hour, but our mind wakes up and wants to move. Or, our mind tells us that eating green vegetables is healthy, but the body (or even the emotions) doesn't want to hear it!

Consider another example. You're supposed to get up in front of the class and give a speech. Your mind knows very well what to do, but your body and emotions don't seem to want to cooperate. Suddenly, you feel nervous and your knees start to wobble!

When things like this happen, it's like we're divided inside. Who is calling the shots? Who gets to decide what happens?

Mindfulness is a skill that helps the different parts of us agree on what to do. It helps us to live harmoniously with our own bodies, feelings, and thoughts.

Brain Power: How Your Mind Can Grow and Change

Our brains and our minds go through phases of development. Small children soak up new information like sponges. In just two or three years, they learn an incredible number of things, including how to move, walk, and talk.

As we get older, it becomes a little more difficult to learn new things. That's because of the brain's way of learning. It's something like creating pathways.

If you've ever walked on a nature trail, or on a pathway on a farm, you will understand how this works. When people keep using the same pathway, the dirt gets trampled down. New grass and plants won't grow there as easily. Because there's a path already, more people go that way, and, over time, the pathway becomes more or less permanent.

The thing is, if we stop using that pathway, over time, it will disappear again. Grass and plants will grow over it, and water might wash some of it away.

Something similar happens in our brains. We create neural pathways (pathways between brain cells). We can strengthen those pathways and make them like deep ruts, but we can also let them disappear.

When we learn something new, like riding a bicycle or playing a musical instrument, we're creating a new pathway in the brain. The more we practice, the easier it becomes. That is true whether it's learning a language, doing homework, or learning a skill. It also counts for learning how to be stressed as a habit, or learning how not to be stressed out as a habit. The more we walk on the "stress" pathway, the deeper the pathway becomes.

If we walk on the "don't stress" pathway more, then that one becomes more permanent instead, and the "stress" pathway begins to fade.

There's a fancy word we can use to name this process. It's called "neuroplasticity," which means our brains and minds are malleable. We can create any kind of shape out of plastic, because plastic is so malleable. Our minds are similar. They change, adapt, and learn things — but they can also unlearn things.

This is why our habits are so important in life. The more we repeat something, the more likely we are to repeat it again. Habits tend to stick, whether they're good habits or bad ones.

Mindfulness uses this feature of the brain to work. Through practicing mindfulness regularly, it becomes a new habit and becomes easier over time. It also starts going deeper, and it can become very rewarding.

Now that we have the basic idea, let's get into it. How do we practice being mindful?

BEMBERTON
BOOKS

SOMETHING FOR YOU

Thanks for buying this book. To show our appreciation, here's a **FREE** printable copy of the "Life Skills for Tweens Workbook"

WITH OVER 80 FUN ACTIVITIES **JUST FOR TWEENS!**

Scan the code to download your FREE printable copy

THE BASIC MINDFULNESS TECHNIQUE

In order to master the art of mindfulness, we will need two things: practice and insight. Both of these are very important.

1. **Practice**. As you will soon discover, mindfulness requires a bit of repetition. Years of habit have trained our minds to *not* be mindful. It's just like learning any new skill — it takes time to rewire your brain and mind. You may think that you're failing at first, and it will probably seem a bit boring, too. Have patience and be wise, because good habits are worth the time they take to cultivate.

2. **Insight**. It's so important to understand *why* mindfulness is good for us. When we see how our own thoughts and feelings have power over us, we gain something invaluable. That insight makes all the difference. It's something that you have to test and confirm for yourself. Otherwise, it's powerless. If you see that it works, you will be naturally motivated to keep practicing. Then, it's no longer a chore. It actually becomes wonderfully calming and energizing.

A Beginner's Guide to Mindfulness: Breathing and Beyond

Let's begin with the first part — how to practice. Once you have some first-hand experience, the insight into *why* it works will be easier.

We're going to explore a number of ways to do the same thing. In this chapter, you will find the basics. In the next chapter, we'll share more about the second part: the insight.

All the different kinds of exercises are useful. They are simply different ways to train our "mindfulness muscles." Different people find different exercises more useful than others. Try them all for yourself and find the ones that work best for you. Choose the ones that feel most natural and fun, and keep practicing.

How to Practice Mindfulness

Before we start, you might find this interesting. It will show you something really important about the way your mind works. Here's a quick way to test it for yourself.

Practicing Mindfulness

Use a stopwatch or timer to time yourself.

The aim is to stay totally in the present moment. Hold your mind steady, watching the timer.
Don't let your mind wander to other thoughts, like "I'm itchy" or "I wonder what's for dinner" or "I must remember to....."
At some point, your mind will get bored or restless. It will then take over and start thinking random thoughts. See how long that takes.

Test yourself to see how long you can just be absorbed by the timer on your phone or watch, and nothing else. The instant you catch your mind wandering off to any thought at all, stop the time.

When you're ready, start the timer.

How long did it take before your mind automatically wandered to something more interesting? Did you forget all about the timer, and then realize with a shock that you were still timing yourself? Whatever your time was, it's fine. It's not a test of your worth! It's simply a way to see something fundamentally true about your mind: Your thoughts and feelings lead a secret life of their own!

Our minds wander all over the place, all the time. We're not *consciously* choosing what to think or feel most of the time. Strangely, we're seldom aware of this important fact. Mindfulness makes us more aware of what's really going on inside us.

We're not going to judge ourselves as good or bad in any way while we practice. We're simply exploring and practicing. There's no goal post. There's no reward system. Forget all about labeling yourself as a success or a failure when it comes to mindfulness. That's counterproductive.

- Try to simply be curious about your own self.

- Stay as open and non-judgmental as possible.

- Try to have fun with it.

- Bring a kind, caring attitude into your practice — that's really important. Be kind to yourself.

Let's explore the simplest, most basic form of mindfulness first. All the other practices are variations on this same theme.

Becoming Aware of Our Thoughts and Feelings

It is helpful for a lot of people to turn mindfulness into a regular practice or exercise. That way, our minds get used to the idea and it slowly becomes a natural part of life. You can adapt this to suit your personal circumstances, but these basics help a lot of beginners.

- You might want to choose a quiet, comfortable place without any distractions.

- It helps a lot of people to sit straight up, either on a comfortable chair or with crossed legs. A straight spine helps the body to relax and the mind to focus.

- Take a few deep breaths, then relax totally and just breathe normally.

- As you're breathing easily, relax more and more deeply into it.

Those are not strictly necessary, but they might help you to get into the "mindful zone." The main thing is to become mindful.

Here's how to do it:

- Think of your conscious power of attention as a torchlight. Wherever you point the light, there your attention goes. Notice the ground under you — that's where your attention is. Notice your own hands — your attention moves there.

- Now, point your attention inwards, back onto itself. (That doesn't mean trying to turn your eyes around and look into your brain. You'll get a terrible headache!) Simply become interested in the one thinking and feeling — in other words, your deeper self. Notice where your thoughts and feelings are coming from.

- *What thoughts are coming and going?* Watch your own thoughts appear and disappear. Do it as if you're watching ships come and go, out on the distant horizon. Spend some time doing that. Don't follow the thoughts. Don't explain them. Don't judge them. Don't grab onto them. Just watch. For instance, maybe the thought comes up "I wonder what Mom is doing downstairs." Notice that thought, but don't pursue it by trying to answer it. There's no need to fight the thought, either. Just ignore it, and it will soon go away. Then, another thought will come, and another...and another. Keep on watching. Don't get involved or feed the thoughts with your curiosity.

- *What feelings are here?* Notice what kinds of emotional feelings are present. There's no need to try to name them or explain them — just pay attention. Even if there aren't any feelings at all, take some time to explore.

- *How does your body feel?* Without needing to give names to the feelings, just notice how your whole body feels. What's it like to be alive in this moment, without a thought in your head? Give yourself time to explore fully.

Some Practical Advice

Start out by giving yourself just a few seconds to explore each part of you. Concentrate, and be as thorough as you can. As you get better at it, extend the time further and further. Challenge yourself to maintain your mindfulness for a minute, then two minutes. Later, once you're comfortable with it, go for five minutes and eventually 10 minutes — or as long as you like!

As you become more mindful, you can start going deeper and deeper. Eventually, mindfulness needs to become a part of life all the time. The practice is just to get us used to the idea. It improves our focus and creates the habit of looking inwards.

Mindfulness slowly creates a quiet, peaceful, and naturally happy atmosphere inside us. It takes a bit of time, and of course practice.

The more you force it, the more you will tense up and get distracted. Instead, try to just allow it to happen. It is helpful if you're really interested and curious about yourself. If you start to relax deeply, that's a good sign! It's working.

The point is to stay present. Be here and now with your thoughts, emotions, and body without needing to explain, judge, or label anything. As soon as you become distracted or forget what you're doing, start over.

Notice what happened. Forgive yourself. Let it go. Relax. After some time practicing, take a break, then try again later. Even if you get distracted a million times, that's fine. Your mindful muscles are growing.

It's actually really simple — it's just paying attention to the here and now, without getting distracted. But when it comes to doing it, it's not always so easy. Most of us struggle to pay attention to our own thoughts for very long.

It helps to have something to anchor our minds in the present moment. The other mindfulness exercises are different ways to do exactly that.

Different Kinds of Mindfulness Exercises

Mindful Breathing

Our own breathing can help anchor us in the present moment. Some people really struggle to watch their thoughts. If that's the case for you, it might help to start by watching something a little more physical. The breath is a great place to focus our attention.

That's because we are able to breathe on autopilot, without thinking about it, but we're also able to breathe on purpose. Here's how mindful breathing works:

Mindful Breathing

☆ While standing or sitting up straight, take a few deep belly breaths. Relax. Get comfortable. (You can also do this lying down, but that might make you sleepy.)

☆ Breathing naturally all the time, just follow your breathing closely with constant awareness. Pay close attention. Become deeply interested in your breath.

☆ As you inhale, notice the feeling of breathing in.
Sense it in your nose.
Explore that feeling.
Now sense it in your whole body.

☆ Notice those quiet moments between each in-breath and out-breath.

☆ Exhale naturally.
Just notice your outgoing breath and relax into it.
Let go of any tension inside you.

☆ Your mind will begin to settle and become quiet.
Thoughts will appear and try to distract you.
That's okay. It's not a problem.
Keep coming back to your breath.
Practice.

☆ You're alive! Feel the truth of this in your whole being.

☆ Keep going—naturally, effortlessly and smoothly.

☆ Use your breathing to stay in the present moment. When thoughts distract you, come back to the breathing, again and again.

☆ Keep practicing. Try to gradually extend the time you're able to breathe mindfully. Start with just one minute for your first attempt. As you get used to it, extend that to two minutes, then five. Eventually you may find yourself getting to 10 minutes. You will find yourself relaxing more and more deeply the longer you can sustain the mindfulness.

ABBY SWIFT

Variations on Mindful Breathing

Just breathing can get boring for a lot of young people (and even adults, too!). There are lots of imaginative ways to tweak this basic mindful breathing exercise. If these methods help you stay mindful for longer, please feel free to use them:

- It helps some people to count their breaths. Beware, though, because you might end up wasting time just counting. It is important to stay present. If the counting helps you focus, use it. If it distracts you, then it's better to drop it.

- Make a humming or buzzing sound on your out-breath. This can also help calm the mind and body. Follow the vibrations from your throat, through your whole body.

- Alternatively, you might want to imagine that, as you breathe in, you're smelling a lovely flower. As you breathe out, imagine you're blowing out a candle.

- Try star-breathing. Make a star shape with one hand by spreading your fingers. Trace the outline with your other hand. As you breathe in, move your finger from your wrist up to the top of your thumb. As you breathe out, trace down the other side of your thumb. Repeat for all your fingers. Then switch hands.

- Include body movements with your breathing. For instance, as you breathe in, bring your hands together in front of your chest, palms together. As you breathe out, expand your hands, like you're expanding a huge balloon. Let your cares float away with those balloons. Release them.

- Energy visualization. Imagine you're breathing energy (chi) in and out as you're breathing. There's a cloud of wonderful colors around you as you're mindfully breathing. The energy fills you up, cleans you, and energizes you. As you breathe out, you're also letting go of stale energy.
- Invent your own variation on this exercise.

Remember, these are just suggestions to make practice easier for you. Try them and find what works best for you. Forget about the other ones — you don't need to master all of them. The idea is to become more mindful, not to master every technique.

Other Kinds of Mindfulness Exercises

You can turn any activity in life into a mindfulness exercise, as we will explain very soon. To get you started, though, here are more mindful practices and ideas to inspire you to explore.

Body Scan

This is especially useful just before you go to sleep or just as you wake up. Lie flat on your back in bed and take five minutes to do a body scan. It helps to place your hands over your stomach area, or palms flat down on the bed. Later, when you are an expert, you might want to extend your time to 10 minutes, 20 minutes, or even more. It's a wonderfully relaxing and healing exercise.

BODY SCAN

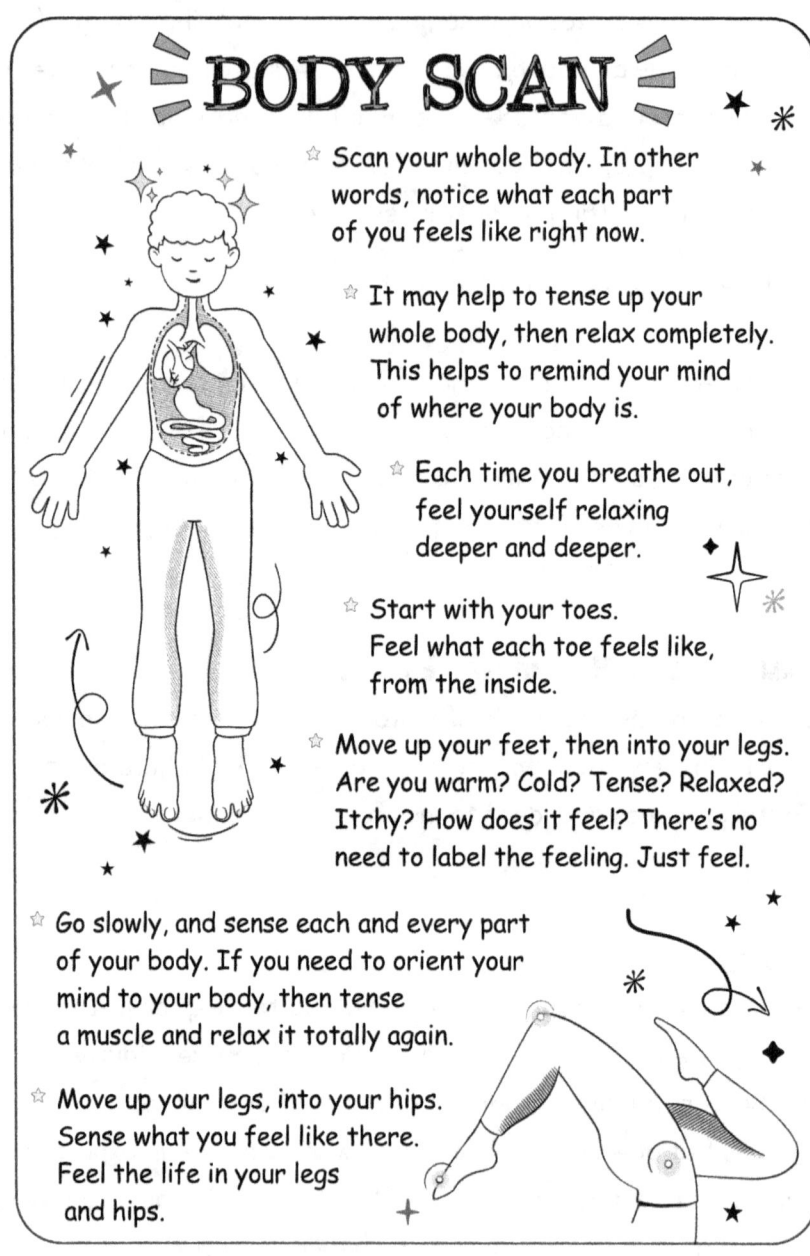

☆ Scan your whole body. In other words, notice what each part of you feels like right now.

☆ It may help to tense up your whole body, then relax completely. This helps to remind your mind of where your body is.

☆ Each time you breathe out, feel yourself relaxing deeper and deeper.

☆ Start with your toes. Feel what each toe feels like, from the inside.

☆ Move up your feet, then into your legs. Are you warm? Cold? Tense? Relaxed? Itchy? How does it feel? There's no need to label the feeling. Just feel.

☆ Go slowly, and sense each and every part of your body. If you need to orient your mind to your body, then tense a muscle and relax it totally again.

☆ Move up your legs, into your hips. Sense what you feel like there. Feel the life in your legs and hips.

☆ Now start moving up your spine, ever so slowly. Feel your stomach and your back, and imagine your organs inside your body. Feel the breath coming in and going out.

☆ Move up the spine to your heart. Feel your heartbeat.

☆ Follow the sensations down both your arms. How do your arms feel? Explore each finger in turn.

☆ Feel your neck, then relax it and relax your jaw completely.

☆ Sense your face and relax your eyes, right up to the top of your head.

☆ Go slowly, sensing each and every part of your entire body. Linger a bit longer on the parts that seem tense or painful.

☆ You might want to imagine you're filling your whole body with honey-flavored medicine light (or any flavor you prefer). You might also want to thank each part of you for being a good friend.

☆ Be kind to yourself while you're doing this. Accept each part of you, just as it is.

A Mindful Heart

Here's another way to do it. This one is simply about focusing on your own heart. It works well for people who are naturally emotionally sensitive (but we can all embrace this skill!).

Mindful Heart

Take a few deep breaths, then relax completely.

Try to sense your heartbeat. If you can't feel it in your chest, put a hand on your heart or find your pulse on your neck or wrist.

Become totally absorbed in sensing your heartbeat.

It's keeping you alive, and life is so interesting. Try to encourage feelings of warmth and gratitude in your heart (emotionally).

Think about something or someone you love, and feel that emotion in your heart area.

Allow that good feeling to expand. Let it fill you up, and fill the whole room, too.

Stay present with it for as long as you can.

These exercises are an excellent place to start your journey into mindfulness. That's not where it ends, though. Our aim is to become more mindful all the time, not just while we're practicing.

Mindfulness can be exercised in just about any part of our lives. When we're walking, we can practice mindful walking. When we're riding a bicycle, we can do that mindfully (provided we stay alert to traffic!). When we're eating, we can do so mindfully. Just about any activity can be made into a mindful exercise.

This helps us transfer what we learn from the exercises into real life — every day.

It is also helpful to know why mindfulness works so well. That's the subject of our next chapter. Once you have tried the exercises in this chapter and start experimenting on your own, the insight will make more sense to you.

INSIGHT: WHY MINDFULNESS WORKS

The thing that makes mindfulness so interesting is that it's so simple, but also so powerful. Oddly enough, it is probably because this technique is so simple that it is also so difficult to master.

That built-in difficulty is also where its power comes from. When we start to use it in everyday life, as a habit, it grows in effectiveness. If it's something we only do once a year at Christmas time, it's not that effective.

Sometimes the simplest things are the hardest to do.

For instance, have you ever tried really hard to fall asleep when you couldn't sleep? Simple, but hard to do. Have you ever made the deliberate decision to live without your phone or electronic devices for a day? These kinds of things are really simple to understand. We might even understand why they're good for us. But still, they are not so easy to do!

Mindfulness is one of those things. We can make the decision to be more mindful. We might even be able to list some of the benefits. That part of it is simple. But it is going to take some patient effort to carry out our decision. Why is that? Let's look a bit more deeply into it.

Mind Power

Our brains, our minds, and the feelings in our hearts are a dynamic force in our lives. "Dynamic," in this case, means they're energetic, versatile, hard to predict, and they change a lot. Our moods and our thoughts can be unpredictable. They influence us in powerful ways.

Are you aware that our minds affect everything we do? The way that we think and the way that we feel affects everything. It changes the way we *react* to whatever happens to us, no matter what that is. It affects every *action* (all the things we do), as well.

That's how powerful your own thoughts and feelings are. They color *everything*. They are a very big part of who you are and how you experience life.

If you have insight into how this is happening right now, you can become wiser, smarter, and happier. You become more mindful.

Know Your Monkey-Mind

Get to know your mind by watching it carefully. Get to know what it likes and what it doesn't like. Notice how it runs away with you, and how it can remain calm. See how it helps you. Try to notice how it trips you up.

Try to become friends with your own powerful mind. Don't let it boss you around. But that being said, there's no need to twist it into impossible knots, either.

Here's something important to know: Our minds like to solve puzzles. They're super active and very creative, which can be a very good thing.

We feel a sense of power when we're able to accomplish something new, especially if it's complicated. We figure something difficult out, and eventually, we get the hang of it. Then we use that skill to make life better. That's the mind's job — and it loves doing it. It enhances the way we feel about ourselves.

An example is the day we learned how to tie our own shoelaces. That was one small but important thing we no longer needed from our parents. Now that we're older, tying our shoelaces isn't all that impressive. Now, we want to learn more complicated skills.

As we grow up, we get more freedom because we become more competent and responsible as human beings. Our minds grow, and we mature. We are able to do more and more things on our own, without supervision. That's a kind of freedom, and a kind of power, too.

Our minds like that kind of experience. It affirms our self-identity. We tell ourselves, "You see! I'm not a loser, I'm not stupid, I'm not a baby. I *can* do it!"

That's wonderful, and it's an important part of life.

The trouble is that our ever-expanding minds can be like restless monkeys. They're not satisfied with what we already know. They constantly want more. They want to move. They get bored easily, and cause trouble. Our clever minds grab our attention and won't let go. That's why our minds distract us from the present moment.

Also, our restless monkey-minds can start to manufacture complicated problems where there are no real problems! That's partly because trouble is hardwired into our survival instincts.

Trouble-Sensing Radar

A big part of the mind's job is to be like a danger-sensing radar. (Radar is a device that scans the horizon for moving objects, like airplanes in the sky, so we know where they are).

The mind scans our environment to find things that might help us or hurt us. That's extremely useful and good for us. In fact, it helped humans develop from cave-dwellers into space station builders.

An alert mind can warn us of traffic dangers. It can also warn us if we're about to injure ourselves or others. It alerts us if we encounter a dangerous situation, so we can be prepared or change course. It's a fantastic feature of the mind.

But it's also troublesome.

A restless and nervous mind *creates* imaginary dangers and resistance to life. It's almost as if the radar is *too* sensitive. It imagines drama where there isn't any. When this starts to happen, it's called anxiety, tension, or nervousness. It's a basic mistrust of our own life situation. Instead of being a good friend, the mind becomes a problem.

This is just like what happened with Ito and the rope that he thought was a snake. In reality, there was no danger, but Ito's imagination got the better of him.

That kind of thing happens far more often than we might believe.

For example, imagine you're sitting and eating your lunch, and some young people nearby start giggling. "They're gossiping," your mind tells you. Instantly, your sensitive mind's radar is on alert. "What if they're talking about me?" Suddenly, you feel self-conscious — and not in a good way. You check to see if you have food on your face or if your zipper is down. In fact, they were laughing about something unrelated to you, but your mind played a trick on you.

Our minds have a habit of creating drama out of thin air — especially when they are restless. We turn tiny issues that are just mole hills into problems that seem like mountains.

That's why we need mindfulness.

It helps calm the restless, mischievous monkeys in our heads.

Our Minds Both Read and Write Our Reality

Here's another important insight that will guide your mindfulness: We take part in creating our own realities. Our minds are incredibly creative, even if we don't think we're creative people.

That's right. We help to create reality. Think about it, and test it for yourself.

Mindfulness helps remind us that we can create a happy reality inside our minds, no matter what is happening outside us.

It's not just the outside world that creates reality. Our five senses tell us what's going on in the world around us. Our brains and minds interpret the signals, which we can then read like a story.

Our complex minds decode a billion signals coming in all the time, and we make sense of it somehow. *We* decide what all these confusing lights, sounds, smells, tastes, and feelings *mean*.

> We also **write** the story of reality in our heads. Here are two examples:
>
> - If we feel small and weak inside, the world looks big and dangerous. If we feel strong and competent inside, the world is no longer so scary. Which world is more real? That depends on you.
>
> - When we compare ourselves to people who have a lot more than us, we seem poor. When we compare ourselves to others who have virtually nothing, we seem quite rich. Which is more real? It depends on you.

The same circumstances and events will affect different people in different ways. Why is that? It's because we have different ways of using our minds. We spin different kinds of stories in our heads about what things mean.

For instance, imagine there are two siblings in the back seat. One sibling might love road trips, and the other might wish it were over already. "Are we there yet?"

They're both in the same place, in the same back seat of the same car. They're related, they're similar, and they share most of their lives together. One person loves the experience, and the other hates it. It's exactly the same situation, but with different minds.

One sibling is creating a wonderful travel story in their mind. The other is creating a boring story.

What kind of reality are you creating for yourself at this moment? Are you aware that you're doing it? That's mindfulness.

Stay Mindful, Stay Happy

It's the simplest thing: Mindfulness means being aware of what we are thinking and feeling. That awareness automatically makes our experience of life richer and deeper. We are able to rise above our own thoughts.

It helps us remember, "I'm creating much of this story in my own head." It gives us the opportunity to think about things in a different way. Our minds are no longer stuck on autopilot mode.

When we're mindful, we might realize that our minds are making life much more complicated than it needs to be. We can see it happening in our minds, and we can simply stop making trouble. We can also notice when our minds are running smoothly and effortlessly.

It's so simple — but it's not necessarily easy. That's because, as we've already discussed, our thoughts and feelings lead a secret life of their own. Our minds are a bit compulsive, like restless, naughty monkeys. They're also good at hiding.

If I tell you, "Whatever you do, don't think of a pink elephant," what's the image in your head? Probably a pink elephant! Random things trigger our thoughts and feelings all the time, and we have little control over them. Thoughts move faster than the speed of light, and one thought jumps to the next without us noticing.

Our thoughts and feelings appear out of nowhere, and it happens lightning fast. We can't help what we think and feel, *but we can become more mindful.*

The moment we become mindful, we create a space around our thoughts and feelings. Those ideas and sensations are not so automatic and compulsive anymore. We have a chance to change our inner reality to a happy one.

Mindful in Everyday Life

This works most powerfully in real life, even more so than in the exercises. For instance, someone may say something insulting about you. How are you going to react?

If you're not mindful at that moment, you'll likely react badly. But if you're mindful, you get to *choose* how you react. You're able to stop and consider where the insult is coming from, without needing to lash out. Perhaps the other person is having a bad day, or is in some kind of pain. You can't know that. Perhaps it's best to just let the insult go, or respond with dignity instead of anger.

Here's another example. Imagine you aren't selected for the team, even though you had your heart set on it. Your mind starts spinning a sad, angry story in your head. "It's so unfair! It was supposed to be me. Why did they choose her instead? What's wrong with me? She must have influenced the teacher. I bet that's what happened."

Without mindfulness, that story becomes your only possible reality. It all *feels* true, so all those thoughts *sound* true, as well. But it might not be true at all — and it's almost certainly not the whole truth.

Mindfulness means catching your mind in the act of spinning that story. "Wait a minute. I don't really know what happened. Maybe it's for the best, after all. Maybe she performed better today. Maybe I could actually improve — and that's not a bad thing."

That's probably the most important thing to learn here.

Mindfulness means being present and aware, at the exact moment the thought or feeling appears.

Afterward, when we've had time to think about things, and when the bad feelings die down, we often regret what we said or did. But the only moment that counts is the moment the thought or feeling actually comes up. That's when mindfulness has power.

What happened has already happened. Mindfulness doesn't change that. What it can do, though, is help us deal with what happened in the most positive way possible — right now.

That gives you a basic insight into why and how mindfulness works. In the next chapter, we will make it more practical and show you ways to apply it in real life.

5

DIFFERENT WAYS TO APPLY MINDFULNESS IN EVERYDAY LIFE

We experience the greatest benefits of mindfulness during real life. We only get a taste of it while we're practicing. The really important stuff happens during all those uncomfortable moments. That's when we actually apply what we know, and when it works its magic.

It happens precisely in the instant we get angry, the very moment we get sad, bored, or anxious, or when we feel a bit worthless. It happens the instant we catch our minds living aimlessly in the past or the future. That's when mindfulness helps us the most.

Sometimes, things happen to us that just aren't fun. That's a fact of life. We all experience moments where we think uncomfortable thoughts and feel uncomfortable emotions. That's quite normal for a human being.

How we react in those moments is what counts.

As we grow up and go through school, with all its many mental, emotional, and social pressures, we can become so focused on just getting through each day that we live in a kind of fog of forgetfulness. We forget to be present in life. We miss the little things that make life special.

Most of us enjoy idling away time on our phones, watching video clips or chatting to friends. We can spend hours doing that kind of thing, without being really present in the moment.

We might spend a whole year doing things like that, trying to avoid what's really going on inside us. Meanwhile, we're often missing what's really happening around us.

We can never get that precious time of life back.

If we're honest, we will notice that we spend much of our lives on autopilot, wishing things were different.

Along the way, we might totally forget to *live in what's really here.*

Mindfulness reminds us to be present in the here and now. We come back into our own skins and fully experience the reality of what's going on. We're no longer going through life like zombies. We're not on autopilot. We're here, engaged in what's happening, no matter what.

Let's look at a few practical examples. Put yourself in someone else's shoes for a moment.

Mindfulness in Action: At School, Home, and Play

Imagine you are on a bus ride to school. There's nothing interesting about it. The same routine happens every day of the school week, with the same people riding along the same boring route. It seems like it takes forever. There's nothing new about it. Or is there?

Today is different, because Candice is being mindful. As she sits in her bus seat, she pays close attention to her breathing. Nobody even knows what she's doing.

A moment before, Candice had been worrying about her math test. Just before that, she had overheard the conversation between the two girls behind her. They were gossiping about the new girl. Candice was about to go off in her mind to revisit all the many problems in her life, both at home and at school, but suddenly she remembered mindfulness.

Candice takes a moment to really be present. She feels her breath coming in and going out. She centers her mind on the present moment.

It's raining lightly. She'd hardly noticed before. She notices a little drop of water running down the bus window, zigging and zagging its way down, and follows it with her eyes. She notices the wet streets below. She hears the bus wheels on the wet asphalt. She notices a young mother driving twins to preschool in the car beside her. They're laughing about something. She can smell the rain and the smells of the bus.

Candice notices the sunlight breaking through the clouds in the sky above for just a brief moment, and for that one instant, she is totally happy and totally at peace.

It doesn't last forever. The next instant, a boisterous young friend sits beside her and starts talking about the crazy thing that happened last night. But something of that peace and contentment stays with Candice for the rest of the day.

How to Calmly Eat an Orange

It's lunch break in a different city and at a different time. Jeffrey is eating an orange, and he's doing it mindfully.

His friends are all on their phones, searching for someone on a social media site. Something scandalous was posted, and they're all trying to find it. Jeffrey isn't interested. At this moment, all that matters is this ripe, juicy orange. He's eating it as if doing so were an artform.

As he peels off the skin, he notices little droplets of juice squirting into the air. He smells the fragrance, and he's present in the moment. He notices the texture of the orange peel. He notices how the segments come apart if he's careful not to break them. He sees the jagged shapes of the peel as he puts them down on the table in front of him.

Jeffrey puts a slice of orange into his mouth and chews. The juice fills his mouth, and he savors the taste. He's eaten many oranges before, but he's never quite noticed the taste the way he notices it now.

Jeffrey is someone who struggles with anxiety. He's a bit of an introvert, and most people at school think that he is a nerd because he likes books and science. He doesn't make friends easily, but the people around this table have accepted him as he is.

In this mindful moment, Jeffrey remembers to accept himself just the way he is, too. He actually likes a lot of things about himself. He suddenly looks around him, as if he has a new pair of eyes.

He notices things that he likes — little details. He sees and hears a jet plane high in the sky above him. He likes that. He notices the shapes of the clouds and the sunlight. He likes sunlight.

He notices some leaves on the grass, blown around by a little swirl of wind. That amuses him, too. He notices the smiles on people's faces. He notices other expressions, too. He realizes that each of the people he sees is probably struggling with something inside them, just like he does. He's not alone.

In this one mindful moment, life isn't complicated, messy, or wrong in any way.

The bell rings, and it's time for English lessons. Jeffrey struggles with those, but do you know what? In this mindful moment, even that doesn't seem like a huge problem. Jeffrey's anxiety is still there, somewhere in the background, but, just for this moment, that's not an issue in his life.

Meanwhile, in a Crowded Home Somewhere

Alicia is on the brink of having a very bad day — the worst.

Her tiny home is always crowded, with four children, Mom, and grandma. Today, it seems like there isn't enough space to breathe. Everything is going wrong. Grandma is still in bed, feeling ill, and Mom has an important job interview, so Alicia has to make breakfast for everyone and clean up afterwards! (Her little brothers never help.)

But her mind is elsewhere. Her grades at school are at an all-time low, and, worst of all, a bad situation is waiting for her today. She has to pass a test at gym class, or she will be penalized. She's been avoiding gym class, and her mother has already been called into the principal's office more than once. Neither of them can handle that today. There's just no way!

Alicia is someone who struggles with body issues because of her weight, and she gets angry a lot. It's her way of coping with her difficult life, but it's not working well. In fact, today, it isn't working at all.

Her little brothers have left squashed cornflakes and milk trails from the table to the kitchen counter, and for Alicia, that's the last straw. She feels that familiar feeling — it's like a volcano is about to go off inside her.

But then — the strangest thing happens. She remembers mindfulness.

Grandma is a wise old lady. She has tried to teach all her grandchildren about mindfulness, with little success so far. For some reason, though, all those lessons suddenly come back to Alicia.

She starts by noticing her body posture. She aligns her head, neck, body, and feet in a straight line. She balances her weight on her feet evenly. She imagines she's growing roots into the ground. Her mind goes quiet and her feelings settle.

Alicia takes a few deep, mindful breaths. She's back in the present moment. All that exists is the here and now.

She notices the sensations in her whole body. That angry energy is there, ready to boil over, but, as she pays close attention, it starts to change!

Alicia suddenly remembers something. When she was little, she loved to dance. Her grandmother used to say, "Aleeshee baby, you sure can skip the light fantastic!" (That was her old-fashioned way of saying Alicia danced like she was walking on air.)

In that mindful moment, the same wonderful light feeling comes back to Alicia. Her body feels full of bright, light energy.

She gracefully wipes up the milk and cereal, like it's a dance. She moves lightly, skipping playfully to the kitchen sink, and starts cleaning the dishes, as if it's part of the performance. Then she starts humming her favorite song, and, for no reason, she starts smiling. In that mindful moment, Alicia accepts herself just as she is. She accepts her life, just as it is. And in that acceptance, she feels a wonderful freedom.

"What's gotten into you?" asks her mother as she rushes through, grabbing her handbag. "Whatever it is, it makes me happy." She gives Alicia a quick hug and says, "I'm late! Remind the boys not to forget practice." Then, like a whirlwind, Mom's out the door with a hasty "Love you!"

All day, Alicia feels wonderful and light inside — for no reason at all. And you know what? Her gym class doesn't go so badly after all.

RIDING THE WAVE OF EMOTIONS: FEELINGS, ANGER, ANXIETY, AND STRESS

Have you ever tried to figure out your feelings? Quite often we can name them, like when we say, "I feel frustrated" or "I'm annoyed," but to actually *explain* those feelings is not easy. We know them quite well, we experience them at different times, we feel them, but we can't always say what they are.

Our feelings are complicated things. It's even possible to feel kind of happy and kind of sad at the same time. That's because our feelings exist midway between our thoughts and our physical energy. They're part body and part mind.

- It's not wrong or bad to feel difficult negative emotions.
- It's not always possible to feel happy, fun emotions.

We can express our emotions in all kinds of ways. Drawing, painting, poems, music, and dance are just some examples. Angry outbursts, nervous shaking, and tears are other examples of ways to express emotions — perhaps not quite as positive or artistic, but powerful nonetheless. Most of us have expressed our feelings in these ways. We each have our own emotional style, just as we each have a unique face.

Remember our illustration about the horse-drawn carriage? Emotional feelings are like those strong horses. They're actually wonderful parts of our lives. Their energy is what gets us moving and keeps us going. They're our inspiration and they pull us along with them.

There's a catch, though. They also have a will of their own, and they don't always obey the driver (the rational mind).

Emotions that feel out of control can be scary. Mindfulness helps us become good carriage drivers. We can become brave and skillful. We can learn how to best harness our emotions and be our own best friends. Instead of fighting ourselves, being angry with ourselves, or being ashamed of who we are, we can learn to get along with ourselves.

> When we're feeling a bit down, it doesn't help to just mentally say, "Cheer up!" When we're feeling anxious, it doesn't help to just say, "Relax!" The mind issues orders, but feelings don't always obey all those orders.

Grappling with Feelings

It takes a whole lot more than a mental instruction to change the way we feel.

Mindfulness helps here, because it goes beyond thinking. We connect with a part of us that is above thoughts and feelings. Or perhaps we can also say that it's *deeper* than our thoughts and feelings. Either way, mindfulness takes us into a space where we can work with emotional energy in healthy ways. We come closer to our true "home base."

Mindfulness creates a space around our thoughts and feelings, and that space is what we need to work with our mental and emotional energies. If there's no space, we act a bit impulsively and compulsively, with little control. Without that calm space, we might end up behaving in ways that hurt us or other people — and we might end up regretting that later.

Bodies and Emotions

We also feel our emotions in our bodies, at least partly. Just as those horses are joined to the carriage by poles and leather straps, our emotions are linked to our bodies. There are all kinds of chemical changes inside our brains and bodies when we feel emotions.

Have you noticed that when people get sad, their body language changes? Their shoulders might slump, their head might hang down, and they might look a bit deflated. When people get angry, the expressions on their faces change. Some go red in the face. Other people might seem to inflate their bodies. Most emotions have telltale signs that appear in our bodies, and especially in our faces.

In fact, changing our body posture can help us manage our emotions better.

Here's an exercise that helps us learn about emotions from our own bodies.

POSTURE MINDFULNESS

☆ Find a place where you can practice privately and in peace, preferably in front of a tall mirror.

☆ Stand up tall, with your shoulders pulled back straight. Don't slouch or slump. Stand firmly, with your spine straight, and puff out your chest just a little - just naturally, without forcing anything. Notice what that looks like. Feel it in your body.

☆ Smile confidently in the mirror. Try to send positive feelings of self-love and acceptance towards yourself. Don't judge yourself as good or bad. Just love yourself as you are. It might feel a bit strange, but try it anyway.

☆ Notice how you feel. Notice how your body feels. Become more mindful of how your body and feelings go together.

☆ Now, do the opposite. Deflate your body. Sag your shoulders down and bow your head a little. Make a sad face in the mirror. It might help to think of something sad.

★ Now, pretend that you're angry. Make an angry face and inflate your body so you look big and scary. You might want to think of someone who annoys you.

★ Notice how you feel.
Notice how your body feels.

★ Experiment with the ways you feel when your body has different postures. Try anxious, or scared, or any other emotions you like. It can be fun to experiment.

★ You will notice that when you're relaxed and natural, you feel much more calm, confident, and positive. Your body language says, "Life is good. I'm happy."

★ As you practice more and more, you will begin to notice it in other people, too. The way they feel is expressed in their body language.

Here's another important mindfulness hack that relates to our bodies and emotions:

- Be mindful of the way you sit, especially when you have to sit for a long time (like when you're in class or in front of a screen). If your posture is good, your default emotional state will feel better in the long run. Are you slouching your shoulders? Are you scrunched up or resting your head on your hands?

  A good posture keeps our head, our shoulders, our body, and our waist in a straight line, more or less. That posture helps keep our spine and back muscles toned and relaxed. That's comfortable, when it becomes your usual habit — and it helps your internal organs work better. Make it a habit.

- Learn to express positive vibes with your body language. Be kind to yourself! Other people will notice and be drawn to you.

There's also a mental side to our emotions. Our brains process the way we are feeling inside, and we explain the feelings in our minds. That's exactly where mindfulness comes in. Let's talk about that next. We're going to explore how our minds and emotions communicate with each other.

Figuring Out Feelings: Why Do I Feel This Way?

We could say that our emotions speak a language of their own. They don't always understand English. They speak a language that we might call something like "Feelinglish."

To deal with them — and to understand them at all — we have to begin to understand this language a bit better. For one thing, we can start to notice our triggers.

Triggers are things that set off our feelings. Here are some examples:

- You lose at a game (or maybe you win).

- Something embarrassing happens to you in front of the class.

- Somebody compliments you.

- Someone gets angry at you for doing something you thought was right.

- People you love are fighting with each other.

- You hear your favorite song.

- You're just plain hungry.

What kinds of experiences trigger your feelings? What makes you angry? What makes you feel embarrassed, nervous, or upset? What makes you feel good? Try to recognize your most common triggers.

Our triggers can be our very own thoughts. For example, consider the thought "I really hate doing this chore!" We think that thought, and immediately we feel an emotion, too — annoyed!

The triggers could be signals from our body, like feeling tired, feeling pain, being hungry, or having indigestion. They could be sympathetic emotions, like when someone else is feeling sad or happy, we might feel that way too.

A big part of mindfulness is becoming aware of these triggers and knowing how we feel when things push our buttons.

Aware of Our Feelings

Without our being aware of it, these triggers might set off our emotional feelings and reactions. The emotional energy wells up inside us and pours out. Once it is on the move, it's hard to stop the flow of emotion. It's as if that carriage driver is shouting "Whoa!" and pulling on the reins, but the horses are ignoring him.

In an instant, our minds try to label our feelings and decide what's happening. But our minds move at a different speed, so sometimes it takes a while to catch up with our feelings. By the time we do, we may have behaved in ways we didn't want to. For instance, we might have said angry words. That might be another trigger for more feelings...like feeling bad about what we said or did.

Step one in managing our feelings is becoming more deeply aware of them as they come up. Step two is using mindfulness to improve matters. Let's use another illustration to make this clear. Imagine you're at the beach. It's a lovely day and the surf's up. There, out on the waves, you see someone with a surfboard.

Surfing Emotional Waves

Jenny loves to surf. She is mindful of the ocean. She paddles out to where the waves break, and then she waits, sitting patiently on her board. She carefully observes the patterns of waves, and when the perfect wave arrives, she's ready.

Paddling like crazy, she catches that wave. Nimble as a cat, she springs up on her board.

In that one important instant, she has to find her balance and stay with it.

For a moment of pure concentration, she gracefully moves as one with that powerful wave — and then it's over. The wave peters out, and she gets off her board. Then she paddles back out again. For Jenny, it's the best feeling in the world.

Riding emotional waves is something like that. We need to be mindful of our ocean of feelings. We can get to know our own patterns of "feeling waves." The instant we feel the wave of energy rise up inside us, we have to act fast. We have to jump up above our thoughts and stay perfectly balanced. That's when mindfulness is most crucial. We need to find our balance in that instant, and stay with it.

If we can stay with that wave of emotion, balancing like a surfer with our awareness, we can change what that wave of energy does to us. It can either sweep us off our balance (and we can lose control of how we're riding our emotions, like behaving badly or lashing out with words), or we can ride it like a pro. We can still feel the emotion, but we don't react thoughtlessly. We measure our words better, we make slightly better choices, and we choose not to hurt ourselves and other people. We surf the moment with grace.

By the way, Jenny wasn't always a good surfer. She had to learn by falling quite a few times — and the same is true of learning to successfully ride our emotions.

Mindfulness doesn't mean fighting our feelings. Most of our discomfort comes from **not accepting what's happening**. That's like trying to surf backwards when the wave goes forwards. Start by accepting what's happening, and work with it — just as it is. If we wish things were different, it's like trying to surf with stiff knees and a rigid body. We will fall off the board. The secret is to relax and flow with the emotion, changing negatives into positives.

Trying to fight and suppress our feelings is like fighting the waves of the ocean. We can't make them go away, and we can't try to stop them with the power of our minds. We need to learn how to ride those waves and *change what they mean*. That way, we behave in healthy ways. We still feel those emotions, but we express them in completely different ways. They don't unsettle us so much, and we don't fall off the surfboard.

That's wisdom, and skillful life-surfing. We can mindfully choose to act and think in different ways, even though the waves of feelings are still there.

It all begins with that cat-like awareness. We train our mindful muscles and learn to wait and watch our ocean of feelings.

We can learn to know what kinds of situations trigger those powerful emotional waves, so that we're ready for them. Then, it takes a bit of balance and practice — and that equals mindfully working with our feelings.

Here's another important thing to understand: When we resist and fight our emotional energy, that's when it feels the most uncomfortable. Because we want to feel differently, we make things so much worse than they need to be. Mindfulness doesn't mean making anger, anxiety, or sadness just disappear. It means moving straight through those emotions smoothly.

When we feel sad, anxious, or bad in some way, what we want most is to feel differently. That's okay — it's normal to feel that way. However, fighting and resisting our emotions doesn't usually work. If we bury our feelings deep inside, they will come back later — and while they're buried, they can hurt us anyway. Fighting and burying emotions usually just adds fuel to the fire. We need to develop the skill to ride our emotional waves in better ways.

Let's explore a few practices that can help us master this skill.

WHAT TO DO WHEN DIFFICULT FEELINGS SHOW UP

This exercise works well for anger and anxiety, but you can use it to work with all kinds of other emotions, too.

Let's split this exercise into two parts. The first part is before or after you feel that wave of emotion. That's when you have time and space to work in peace. The second part is during the wave. That's more difficult, because you're already in the moment.

Before and After the Waves

Jenny learned to sit on her board and watch the waves. She got to know the ocean and its ways. That's a useful way to think about our emotions, too.

Take some time to regularly practice being mindful of your emotions. This way, you get to know your feelings better in a calm, peaceful space. Practice when the waves are small, and you'll be ready for those crucial moments when they feel uncomfortable. Then, when the moment comes, paddle quickly on your "mindfulness surfboard" and catch your balance. First, though, while you're calm — and while there's no pressure — you can practice balancing. Here's how:

☆ Find a quiet place where you feel comfortable, happy, and relaxed.
Make sure there aren't too many distractions.
Switch any mobile devices to silent.

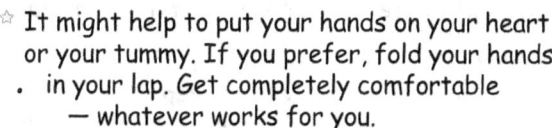

☆ Sit comfortably with your spine straight and take a few deep breaths.
Three or four deep breaths will do nicely.

☆ Bring your attention together and focus on your center.
Forget about the outside world for just five minutes.

☆ It might help to put your hands on your heart or your tummy. If you prefer, fold your hands in your lap. Get completely comfortable — whatever works for you.

☆ Notice how your whole body feels, and relax more and more deeply as you calmly breathe. Be present in the here and now. Take some time and settle deeply into it.

☆ Investigate the body sensations in your stomach and heart area.

☆ Try to become aware of what kinds of emotions are present with you right now.

☆ It helps some people to name those feelings, like "bored" or "restless," but that isn't always possible. The important thing is to recognize them in your own way.

☆ Is your body tense? Where?
Is it relaxed? Is your heart beating?
How does it feel?

☆ Allow whatever is here to be here.
Accept the way you feel, exactly as it is.
Be kind to yourself.

ABBY SWIFT

☆ Be genuinely interested in how you feel.
Explore it carefully and take your time.

☆ Are you anxious at all?
Are you worried about something?
Do you feel hot or cold?
Are you feeling restless?
Are you angry in any way? Sad?
Is your mind resisting you?
Whatever is happening, be curious about it.

☆ Accept whatever is happening in this moment, just as it is.

☆ Try to encourage a warm, open, and accepting feeling deep inside you. If you feel the stirrings of a peaceful, happy feeling deep down, then encourage it to open up. If not, just sit and watch patiently. Try not to force anything. Just relax and be totally present.

☆ There's no need to judge anything, especially not yourself.

☆ Notice how your mind wants to jump in and explain everything. That's fine — just watch it and keep coming back to your center, exploring your feelings directly.

LUCKY THE WAY I AM

☆ When you're in the zone, or even just close to it, say to yourself, "I'm alive, and switched on. I'm okay, just the way I am."

☆ Make it a habit to practice regularly.

Why does this help? It helps because our deeper (mindful) awareness changes the way our minds label and interpret our feelings. As we become more aware of the feelings inside us, we get used to how that feels, and we reinforce the habit of interpreting that in a positive way.

When we don't learn how to be mindful, we can easily reinforce negative habits instead.

Worrying makes our bodies tense. Tense bodies make us feel worried again, which in turn makes us feel tense. That's a loop that keeps us stuck feeling anxious. Mindfulness of our emotions helps to break that cycle and trains us to create helpful loops instead.

One of the best antidotes is to simply relax as deeply as possible — on a regular basis.

Mindfulness helps us get there, and then helps us remember how that feels. It becomes our habitual body-memory. It's similar to the way our bodies remember how to ride a bicycle.

Our bodies can help to remind us of what "just relax!" actually means in practice. (Our minds are not that good at relaxing!)

During the Waves

This is the most difficult part of mindfulness, but it's also where it has the most positive effects. For both of those reasons, it takes the most practice to master.

Usually, when strong emotions come up, we're really *not* mindful at that moment. That's when we can easily lose our balance and self-control. Practicing before and after this happens helps make mindfulness a habit, and eventually we are able to be more mindful when that big wave comes.

As much as possible, try to be present when you experience a strong wave of emotion. The moment it happens, you need to be ready to jump up onto the surfboard. How?

- Recognize what's happening. Say to yourself, "I'm starting to feel anxious" or "I'm getting angry" (or whatever other feeling comes up).

- Become deeply aware of the wave of emotion that is flowing inside you. Notice how it feels. Notice how your body feels. Notice how your breathing changes. Notice if you feel hot, cold, prickly, or whatever else you experience.

> **What's important is to look at it in a kind way. Wrap it in love. Surround it with friendly acceptance. Give it room to breathe. Give it lots of space. Shine your light of wisdom into it and bring it out into the open.**

- Become deeply aware, and be present. "I'm here. I get to choose what I do next."

- Understand that fighting the wave is counterproductive. Instead, accept it and rise above it, balancing by means of your awareness of the feeling. Don't get swept off the surfboard, if you can help it.

- Express your feelings in the best way that you can. You don't have to be perfect — just try to do your best in the moment.

For instance, you might say, "I know I'm feeling angry right now. I'm aware of the feeling, and I am going to express it in the best possible way, without hurting myself or anyone else."

Here's another example: "I am starting to feel very anxious. I'm aware of it. Anxiety is not my enemy, and I don't have to let it ruin my day. It's actually quite interesting. I don't have to give in to my fear. My fear is actually here to help me be careful and wise."

Here are some more tricks and techniques that can help with strong emotions in the moment.

Move energy inside you. It might help to move the energy around in your body, since emotions are linked to body feelings. For instance, you could raise your arms above your head for 30 seconds.

If you're filled with uncomfortable energy and it feels like that excess energy needs to come out, then try jumping up and down in one place. If you don't like that kind of thing, then do a silly dance or move the energy in a way that feels right in your own body. Walk, run, sing, or laugh — whatever works for you and doesn't harm anyone else in the process.

Just breathe (with awareness). Breathing mindfully is another powerful way to come to grips with anxious feelings that seem as if they're going to overwhelm us. This helps when we're sitting on a bus or in class and we can't move physically to get that feeling out. It even helps when we're out in the open air. Your breath is always with you. It's a friend and a lifeline.

Focus on breathing in, then holding for two seconds, then breathing out. Forget *everything* else. Repeat, repeat, repeat. Fill your mind only with breathing, and feel yourself come back down to earth.

Literally feel the ground underneath you. Sense your own feet pressing down into the ground. The ground is still there, holding you up. You're okay. You're a part of nature, and are going through something natural. There is great wisdom in nature. It will be okay in the end — and even if it's not okay right now, it's not the end.

Know that the feeling will pass. You're bigger than this experience. It's temporary, and you will still be okay once it has passed.

Be kind and curious. Kindness and curiosity are two wonderful ways to cope. Try to be kind to yourself, and curious about what is happening. Remind yourself, "It's okay to feel this way. I get to choose the best way to act right now. I wonder what is possible right now?" That helps to open up the door that the emotion has shut. Curiosity opens up our minds. Kindness opens up our hearts.

Forgive. If the wave of emotion sweeps you off balance, don't make things worse by being angry with yourself or feeling disappointed. Forgive yourself. And if you were unkind to someone else, explain what happened and ask them to forgive you, too. Then paddle back out and get ready for the next wave.

Practice. Practice. Practice. Even if you fail most of the time, don't give up. Gradually, you will become more emotionally mature, and one day you'll be surfing emotions like a pro!

These strategies are things that you will need to experiment with over time. You can keep coming back to this chapter to remind yourself of things you may forget. At first, it might all seem a bit complicated and messy. It may seem as if you are never going to get your balance on that wave of emotion. But don't give up.

To help you even more, especially in the beginning, here's a simplified version of what we've discussed already. It's called the "RAIN" method, and it's easy to remember.

As the old saying goes, "When it rains, it pours!" Sometimes, a lot of bad things seem to happen all at once, as if they're all pouring down on our heads. Bad experiences can feel like rain that never ends — one thing after another. Take courage! Even these experiences will pass, like the clouds — and there's sunshine on the other side. The following technique might help during those "rainy" times.

Each letter in the word "RAIN" stands for one part of what we've already talked about. It goes like this:

The RAIN Technique

RECOGNIZE

Notice the feeling as it is, even if you can't put a name to it.

ACCEPT

Acceptance means acknowledging the feeling without necessarily agreeing with or liking it.

INVESTIGAGE

Explore the feeling further. Reflect on why you might be experiencing it.

NON-IDENTIFICATION

It may seem unusual, but it's important not to define yourself by the feeling.

- **Recognize**: When you notice a strong emotion bubbling up inside you, take a moment to recognize it. Say to yourself, "I'm feeling angry" or "I'm feeling sad." Acknowledge the feeling just as it is, even if you can't name it. "I'm feeling something."

- **Accept**: Instead of pushing the feeling away or pretending it's not there, accept it. It's okay to feel what you're feeling. Acceptance doesn't mean you agree with the feeling or like it; it just means you're acknowledging it. "This feeling is on the bus with me. That's okay, there's room for everyone."

- **Investigate**: Dive a little deeper into the feeling. Ask yourself why you might be feeling this way. Maybe something happened at school or with friends that triggered the emotion. What is it doing in your body? How does your heart feel? Remember, you get to decide what the feeling means. That's your power.

- **Non-identification**: It might sound weird, but it is important that you don't identify yourself as the feeling. Remember that you are not defined by your emotions. The feeling is definitely there — but it's *not you*.

Just because you're feeling angry doesn't mean you're an angry person. Just because you're feeling sad, anxious, or whatever else doesn't make you that person. Recognize that emotions come and go, like clouds in the sky. That's what we mean when we say that mindfulness makes "space" around our thoughts and feelings. You're like the sky. The feeling is like a cloud. It will pass.

Give yourself some space. By practicing the RAIN method, you're giving yourself space to breathe and respond to your emotions in a healthy way. It's like putting on a raincoat during a storm — it helps you weather the difficult moments with a little more ease.

Mindfulness helps us take it easy through life, and that's especially helpful for those of us who struggle with anxiety — which is the subject of our next chapter.

MINDFULLY COPING WITH STRESS

It has been said that dogs are a human's best friend. Are you a person who loves dogs? Most dogs are wonderful friends and companions. Some dogs are marvelous helpers, like guide dogs and watchdogs. But with other dogs, it's a different story. The only things they watch are the food bowl and the cupboard where the snacks are kept. And then there are those dogs that just can't stop barking.

Our minds can be a bit like that, too. They can be wonderful friends and marvelous helpers, but they can just as easily keep us awake all night with their nervous yapping.

Fear is there to be a friend and a helper. It's meant to be like a trusty watchdog. Fear is vigilant and alert. It warns us when something isn't right. But anxiety and stress are a different kind of watchdog. They just won't keep quiet and leave us in peace!

Anxiety and stress happen when our fear isn't doing its job in the right way. We keep getting urgent warning messages, and we can never relax. Remember what we said about our minds being like trouble-sensing radars? That's a big part of it. When we're stressed, our radars don't switch off. They're constantly beeping: "Danger, danger."

Often, that's because we're not responding properly and taking action. Other times it's just a glitch in the system.

Our bodies respond to those warnings by releasing chemicals called cortisol and adrenaline. These chemicals are good for us when we need to react fast — like when we need to run or get out of the way — but they are very bad for us when we need to relax, sleep, or study for a test. If those chemicals show up when we need to give a speech in front of the class, they can be downright incapacitating. They make our knees shake and our voices go funny. That's anxiety.

Mindfulness helps us use our fear in a good way. It helps us relax more quickly after a warning, and keeps our body chemicals more balanced, too. That's very good for our health.

A big part of fear's job is to make us wake up and pay attention. Practicing mindfulness actually makes us more aware of what's going on, and that helps us manage our fear in a healthy way. We're no longer nervously scanning our surroundings for danger — we're simply paying attention in a calm, sustainable way. That makes all the difference.

Let's look at how to mindfully deal with stress and anxiety.

Spotting Stressors and Understanding Why They Bug You

What are stressors?

Stressors are things that cause stress in our lives. They can be big things, like tests at school, arguments with friends, or feeling overwhelmed with chores. But they can also be smaller things that add up over time.

It helps to understand your reactions. Sometimes, stressors can make us feel upset, angry, or worried. For example:

- Tests and homework: Feeling nervous before a big test or overwhelmed by a pile of homework can definitely be stressful. You might worry about doing well or meeting deadlines.

- Friendship drama: Arguments or misunderstandings with friends can leave you feeling upset and stressed out. You might worry about losing a friend or not fitting in.

- Family tension: Family disagreements or changes at home, like moving to a new house or parents divorcing, can also be stressful. You might feel torn between family members or worry about how changes will affect your life.

- Feeling pressure: Sometimes, you might feel pressure to do well in sports, clubs, or other activities. This pressure can come from yourself, parents, teachers, or coaches, and it can add to your stress.

Keep a stress journal: One way to figure out what stresses you out is to keep a stress journal. Write down things that bother you and how they make you feel. You might want to briefly explain the circumstances. More importantly, explore how it makes you feel inside. This helps you to understand how you're reacting inside to the circumstances around you.

Here's an example: "Today Mom looked very stressed out, and that stressed me out, too. She says everything is going to be okay, but I know we're struggling with money. I've been wanting to ask her about getting me a new phone, but I decided not to add to her troubles. That makes *me* worry even more! I don't like feeling this way. Will it ever end? I'm going to keep doing my best at school and help out as much as I can around the house, but I have so many things of my own to do!"

Understanding your stressors and how they make you feel is one important step in learning how to cope with stress.

How does identifying the stressor help? It helps because bringing the light of awareness into anxiety starts to dissolve the anxiety.

It helps us to accept what we're going through, and to work with it in an open and honest way. Then, it's easier to be courageous about stress.

Remember Ito and the rope-snake? As soon as the candlelight revealed that it was a rope and not a snake, Ito calmed down. It's the same with little children who are scared of monsters under the bed or in the cupboard. If a parent looks under the bed and in the cupboard, the child is less afraid. It's what we aren't aware of that scares us most. When our feelings are hiding in the dark, they can affect us much more than when those feelings are out in the open.

Bringing awareness to anxiety helps us get over the fear of the unknown. If you look carefully into your anxiety, you will see that much of it hinges on being afraid of something unknown.

By identifying what stresses you out, you can start to find healthy ways to manage your feelings and take care of yourself. You can take practical steps to deal with what you *know* is coming.

Your Stress Toolkit: Mindful Methods to Keep Calm and Carry On

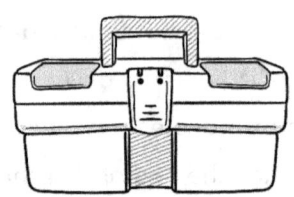

Have you ever noticed that the more we worry about something, the bigger and scarier it seems to get? It's like feeding a hungry monster — the more we feed it, the stronger it becomes. But what if I told you that you have the power to stop feeding those anxious feelings?

Imagine your emotions as hungry creatures. When we give them our attention and energy, they grow bigger and louder. For example, if we constantly worry about something, like a big test or a difficult conversation, we're actually feeding our anxiety and making it stronger.

Breaking the cycle: The good news is that we can break this cycle by changing the way we respond to our emotions. Instead of being worried about being worried, we can learn to create space around our feelings and stop feeding into them. It's like taking away the monster's favorite snack. Without our attention, it starts to shrink and lose its power.

Mindfulness in action: Mindfulness teaches us to be present in the moment and observe our thoughts and feelings without judgment. When we notice ourselves getting caught up in anxious thoughts, we can gently bring our attention back to the present moment. Here's how:

- **Check in with your body:** Take a moment to tune in to how your body feels right now. Notice any tension or discomfort, and see if you can soften and relax those areas. If you can relax your body more, the anxiety becomes less overwhelming. Move, sing, or do something that helps your body calm down. Breathing is a good way to do this, too.

- **Focus on your breath:** Pay attention to your breath as it flows in and out of your body. Notice the rise and fall of your chest, or the sensation of air passing through your nostrils. Your breath is always with you, serving as an anchor to the present moment.

- **Check your posture:** Notice how you're sitting or standing. Are you slouched over or sitting up straight? Adjust your posture to feel more open and confident. Sometimes, simply changing your physical stance can help shift your mindset.

- **Relax your face muscles:** Often, when we're stressed, we hold tension in our faces without even realizing it. Take a moment to relax your forehead, unclench your jaw, and soften your eyes and cheeks. Notice how this simple act of relaxation can help ease tension throughout your body.

- **Feel the flow:** Experiences, circumstances, and events come and go like water in a river. No single event lasts forever. Whatever is making you anxious will eventually pass, just as water passes through a river. A big part of anxiety is how we resist the flow of experiences. Instead, feel the flow. Being tense and fighting the flow of events will not help you or make you safe. Working with the flow will help. Get comfortable with the coming and going of strange new experiences, and flow with them instead of fighting them. Use that energy to do something useful, rather than resist.

By incorporating these mindful practices into your daily life, you can build resilience against stress and cultivate a sense of calm and balance, even in challenging moments. Remember, you have the power to choose where you direct your attention, so why not feed your sense of peace and well-being instead?

THE REAL "ME" VERSUS MY IDEAS ABOUT ME

Here's something every wise young person needs to understand clearly: You can exist without your thoughts, but your thoughts cannot exist without you. Don't let your thoughts take over and run your life without your permission. The real you comes first. Your *thoughts* about you come second.

Consider the fact that in deep sleep, there isn't a thought in your head, yet you are still alive. You still exist.

Or, think about those wonderful moments in life when you see something beautiful, awesome, or startling, and your mind goes absolutely quiet. You're still there, awake and present. The thoughts have gone, but *you* remain.

In fact, without all those noisy thoughts and feelings, the moment is even better. Your senses work better and you can absorb more.

> *The feeling of being "me," knowing that I exist, just as I am, here and now — comes before thinking.*
>
> *Just being me is more important, and more powerful than any single thought, or feeling, or experience I might have.*

Mindfulness means seeing this truth and remembering it, then putting things back into their proper place.

Thoughts and feelings are not problems, but they can become problems when they're not in their proper place. That happens when we forget that they are merely thoughts and feelings.

Here are a few examples of thoughts that grab hold of us in this way: "Life is too hard," "I will never succeed," "Everyone is judging me," and "I'm all alone."

If bad things happen to us, we might think, "Why is this happening? My life is just too difficult!" In that instant, we forget all about the rest of our lives. That one thought, "life is too difficult," and that one bad experience becomes all that exists as real and true. They become all-important. That thought takes hold of us in a powerful way. It gains power over us, and that's not the proper place for any thought or any feeling.

When we're *not* mindful, our thoughts and feelings have a way of taking over. It's as if they are sitting in the driver's seat of our lives. They pretend to be the boss of us, and they can fill our days with all kinds of troubles. They take us wherever *they* want.

When we are mindful, those thoughts and feelings are still there, but they sit in the back seat of the car and behave. They may be noisy, but they're not making our decisions. They're not driving the car. They simply appear in that back seat for part of the journey.

Negative thoughts appear, but they are not you. Sad experiences happen, but they are not you. Angry thoughts and feelings appear, but they are not you. Difficult circumstances may come about, but they are not you, either.

Remember the RAIN method? The letter "N" stands for non-identification. That means not identifying with our negative thoughts. For example, we might have the thought "I'm not good enough." Instantly, we feel like a person who is not good enough, because we have identified with the thought. It has become who we are.

Non-identification switches that negative thought to a positive: "*What I did* wasn't what I wanted to do" or "*The way I behaved* could have been better." Do you see the difference? The negative thought means you're not good enough. The more positive thoughts mean you *are* good enough, although your behavior could change in a positive way.

You are not the thoughts in your head. You are not the circumstances that happen to you. You are, however, the one who lives through them all and comes out intact on the other side. Not one of those things can define you. Not one of them can destroy you. You're bigger than all of those things put together.

Who Am I? Exploring Your True Self with Mindfulness

Mindfulness helps us to discover a depth of "being me" that our thoughts don't reach. We discover a silent place inside us where thoughts no longer grab our attention and run away with us.

In that quiet, peaceful, happy place, your real self can breathe. You can come out of your shell and explore who you really are. You don't need to explain it. You can just be it.

Right now, you're thinking, so use this opportunity to think about the one you call "me." This person that we each refer to as "I" — who is that person, really?

Is it your name? Is your name all that you are? No. The fact that you were born as a boy or a girl — is that all that you are? No, it isn't. Are your parents all that you are? Of course not. What about your nationality, or your age, or your favorite seat on the bus? None of those things is you.

What about your body? If you cut your hair or trim your nails, does "you" disappear? Of course not. As your body changes when you grow up, deep down, don't you still feel like your same old self?

No matter what happens to you, there in the background is the same familiar feeling of being yourself. It never goes away. "I am what I am." Just that is so much more than enough.

Each of these things, like your name, gender, and nationality, says something about who you are, but not one of them tells the whole story. The real, deepest "you" is so big that it contains everything that you will ever feel, ever think, and ever experience. Yet, when we look for that elusive "I" with our minds, it is very hard to find.

Mindfulness takes us right there. It brings us into a wide open space, where we can just be alive, free, and peaceful, exactly as we are. There's nothing to add, and nothing can be taken away.

That's super useful, because we can so easily become stuck on labeling ourselves. We might even believe hurtful or painful things about ourselves.

Silencing the Inner Critic Without Hitting Mute

Mattheus often overhears a conversation in his own thoughts. It goes something like this: "I'm such a loser. All the other kids got it right the first time, or the second, but I have tried a hundred times, and still I can't do it. What's wrong with me? I guess I'm just useless, and that's how it's going to be for life."

That voice isn't always there, but it appears quite often. Mattheus struggles with math. He also struggles with science and biology — and most other subjects too. His brain seems to work a little differently, and he hasn't figured it out yet. What he forgets, though, is all the things he's really good at. He can run faster than people who are two or three years older than him and bigger than him. He's really artsy, and he can make just about anything out of wood, clay, scraps of metal, or whatever else he finds. He's good with languages, too. And lots of people like him. Mattheus often forgets all those things, and all he hears is that one nagging voice.

Genie has her own inner critic. Inside her head, it sounds a little different. "Why doesn't anybody like me? What am I doing wrong? I was so nice to her, and she just ignored me. All of them do! Why doesn't anyone want to be my friend? I'm a nice person, aren't I? I guess not...."

Martha criticizes herself because she comes from another country, and struggles to fit in. In her head, there's another voice that keeps saying things like: "People here are so different from what I'm used to. They all think I dress funny. Just look at their faces when I open my lunch! They must all think I'm such a weirdo! I'm never going to fit in. I'm going to be an outsider for my whole life. I'll probably turn into an old cat-lady and live alone forever."

These people are struggling with their inner critics. An inner critic is a voice or a feeling inside us that tells us negative things about ourselves. It lists all our faults, and it's often quite merciless. It knows exactly which buttons to push to make us feel really, really bad about ourselves.

There's actually a part of that critical inner voice that's good for us. That's probably why most of us put up with it.

The voice of our inner critic helps us to see our own faults, and work at improving them. It helps us hear the voice of our own conscience, which prevents us from hurting ourselves and others. It pushes us to improve and to grow. Those are all good and positive things. However, there's a downside.

Those negative thoughts and feelings can become compelling, and even addictive. They can become constant and overwhelming. We might start to believe that those negative thoughts and feelings are the *only* true things about us.

They might sound and feel so true that we forget all about our good qualities. Our minds might be pulled only to the negatives, like a compass needle to a strong magnet.

Mindfulness helps us detach from our inner critic long enough to put things into perspective. Each of us has good and bad qualities. What's important is this moment, and how we show up for life right now.

"Selfie"-Esteem: Building a Picture of the Real, Awesome You

Deep inside you there is a mystery of great value. It's the feeling of truly being you.

Our negative thoughts about ourselves have their place. After all, how can we change things about ourselves that aren't working if we are not aware they aren't working? The thing is, it's not necessary to keep hanging on to those negative thoughts and feelings. Note them, work on them if you can, but then move on.

Once we become aware of what needs to change, we can start doing just that. It might take a lot of time, but there's no need to keep beating ourselves up along the way.

Signs that you're struggling with your self-image include never wanting to try new things (especially if you think you won't succeed), difficulty speaking to other people, and frequently feeling frustrated with yourself. One of the biggest signs is if you notice that you're often speaking to yourself in a negative way.

Here are some mindful ways to build a healthy picture of the real, awesome you.

- **Write a friendly letter to yourself**. Imagine your best friend has moved to a faraway city, and that friend is struggling. Write a friendly letter, encouraging your beloved friend to keep on going, and to stay in touch. Remind them of the good times you had together, and promise them that you'll always be there. Make them laugh. Make them smile. Let them know you care. The only difference is — that friend is none other than *you!*

- **Keep a memory box**. Collect little reminders of times when you feel really good to be alive, and when you are happy to be you. Maybe it's a ticket stub to an event, a little stone, a sticker, or something else. Associate that object with the good feelings you have about being you.

- **Make a list or journal of things you love about you**. It might be your sense of humor or the way you dance. Maybe it's your skill at making silly poems or skipping a stone across the pond. Whatever you love about being you, add that to the list. Check in from time to time, and keep adding small things, no matter how insignificant they may seem. When you're feeling down, you can always look at that list and remember the upside of being you.

Here are some prompts to get you started:

- Something unique about me is...
- Today something pretty cool happened...
- I feel most proud of myself when...
- Although things are tough right now, I decided to...
- What I actually like about me is...

NAVIGATING LIFE'S BIG CHANGES

Navigation is a useful skill to learn. Are you one of those people who has a faulty sense of direction? Some people seem to always know which way is north, but not all of us are like that. The rest of us need Google Maps.

Most of us know what it feels like to lose our way. Perhaps it happened when you were still a small child, or maybe more recently. Can you remember how it felt to be lost?

It's a scary feeling. Suddenly, everything looks unfamiliar. Our minds try to orient themselves, but we can't remember which way is which, and we're not sure which way to go. The further we go, the more lost we get. Sometimes, that same feeling even visits us in our dreams. We might start to panic a little bit, or at least feel terribly frustrated.

The same kind of feeling can come to us when our world changes.

When we change schools, move to a new home, have to make new friends for some reason, or lose someone — any major change in life — we might feel a bit lost. It's scary, and it's uncomfortable. It can even make us start to stress out or become sad. We might long for what we used to have. It's like there's a hole in our heart somewhere, and we feel small, fragile, and well lost.

As we grow up, all kinds of things change — and it's not always easy to handle a world that keeps on changing.

There's bad news and there's good news. The bad news is that change will continue to happen all throughout your life. Change is a basic part of the nature of things. The good news is that change does not actually have to be scary, or your enemy.

Without change, would life even be possible at all? If nothing changed, nothing could grow. Nothing new could be born, including you. If nothing ever changed, there wouldn't be day or night, seasons, or any kind of movement at all. That's not life, because life means change, and life is a good thing. In other words, change is actually our friend.

Mindfulness helps us to use our own inner compass to navigate change. We can orient ourselves more easily, both mentally and emotionally, and find our way. When we become skilled at being mindful, we know which way to go, no matter what happens or where we find ourselves. Mindfulness helps us embrace change.

New School, New Rules: Finding Your Feet with Mindfulness

Jasmine is sitting alone on the steps. It's just after school, and she's waiting to be picked up. There are a few people around, but none of them are speaking to her.

She's in a new school, and she's not used to her new home yet. Everything's in the wrong place. Jasmine feels lost.

Her parents had to move because of work—this is the fourth time they've had to move cities! Jasmine hates it. As soon as she makes friends, she has to move again. This time will probably be no different.

As she's waiting, Jasmine thinks about what she can do to pass the time. She's about to reach for her phone, when another idea strikes her. She remembers mindfulness.

Jasmine takes a few long, delicious breaths and settles into her center. She makes her spine straight and closes her eyes.

That helps her focus. Then, she just notices the breaths coming in and going out. For a minute and a half, she does nothing else. Soon, she starts to relax deeply.

She notices her whirling thoughts about school and her new home. She notices the emotions she is feeling — frustrated and alone. Then, she becomes curious about those feelings, and watches them carefully. She makes a space around them.

Jasmine acknowledges those thoughts and feelings, and remembers what they are. They are just thoughts and feelings. "They will pass," she silently tells herself. Suddenly, it seems to happen all by itself. The feelings and thoughts are still there, but now they're off somewhere in the background. Jasmine slowly becomes so relaxed that she completely forgets where she is.

"What are you doing?" someone asks suddenly, and Jasmine is startled. She smiles shyly and looks a bit embarrassed. A friendly girl from one of her classes is asking the question. She looks genuinely interested.

"You seem so calm!" laughs the girl. "Like you were meditating or something. I always wanted to try that. Can you teach me?"

Just like that, Jasmine's whole day has changed. She's made a new friend, and life doesn't seem so bleak anymore.

Jasmine knows that, just like all her many other friends, she might eventually end up having to switch to a long-distance relationship with this new friend. But that's okay. In this moment, there's an interesting conversation to be had and a whole new person to get to know. That's perfect for now.

Friend Flux: Making and Keeping Friends Through Ups and Downs

Being a friend means many things. It means spending time with someone. It means getting to know them and accepting them for who they are. It means listening and being open to their crazy ideas without judging them, even though you don't agree. It means caring and helping your friend when they need you. It means keeping them in your heart.

That's also true about making friends with *you*.

Mindfulness starts with you. Mindfulness means regularly spending time with the real you. It means getting to know who that really is. A big part of mindfulness means accepting yourself as you are, deep down. It means listening and paying attention, without judging. It means being kind to you, through your ups and downs.

That's the very best place from which to work when it comes to making and keeping friends. Deep down, other people are a lot like you.

Mindfulness helps make us compassionate. We start to care more about other people. It happens because, first of all, we care about ourselves. Then, we begin to see that, just like us, other people struggle with difficult thoughts and feelings, too. If we know how to be a friend to ourselves, we can also learn how to be a good friend to others.

It's like our hearts are these big wellsprings of love energy. When our hearts are empty, there's nothing to share. When we fill our hearts with love, they overflow and we can't help sharing good feelings with the people around us.

Make sure your wellspring is full. That starts by loving yourself unconditionally. When your heart is full of love, you will inevitably want to share it with others, whether they consider you a good friend or not.

That's how mindfulness can help us navigate the ups and downs of complicated friendships.

Body Talk: Being Okay with Changes During Tween Years

Jason stares into the bathroom mirror, and he's not happy. He thinks to himself: "Have aliens from another planet switched me into something weird overnight? How am I supposed to love myself when I don't even recognize the face in the mirror anymore? Where on earth did all those spots come from? And I'm sure that my knees aren't where they used to be!"

Mindfulness has helped Jason through some tough times, so he tries it now. Even though he's not completely happy with the way his body looks on the outside, he turns his attention inwards in a mindful way.

He stands up tall and makes his posture confident and relaxed. He breathes deeply a few times, then scans his whole body on the inside. Yes, he's still alive. He can feel the life in his toes, in his legs, and all the way up his body. He can feel warmth in the palms of his hands, and he can follow the feelings all the way up to the crown of his head. He begins to relax and to completely accept this moment, just as it is.

Jason opens his eyes and looks into the mirror again. Sure enough, the spots are still there. But now there's a different feeling inside him. He can remember looking into the mirror so many times growing up, watching himself grow and change. That same boy is still inside here. He's still the same guy. Jason actually loves that little guy. He takes some time to settle and stay mindful. He makes peace with the moment, just as it is.

"Okay, ugly spots," Jason smiles into the mirror. "I don't have to like you, but I accept that you're here. I'd like you to move on as soon as possible, if that's okay, but you're not going to ruin my life. You guys won't be here in a couple of years, but I will still be here. So there's that, at least."

Jason washes his face and gets ready to go to school. Not everything that happens to him that day is perfect, but he makes it through and he's okay with being Jason.

Making Friends with Change

Events, happenings, circumstances, and situations fill up our whole lives, and they're constantly on the move. Each new moment brings a fresh surprise, and eventually everything changes. The best way to cope is to make friends with change.

Ships have heavy anchors that keep them from drifting away on the tides and the waves. Mindfulness can be like your anchor during those times when change happens.

Why? Because through mindfulness we find a space inside us that is not affected by time or change. It's always the same. Mindfulness anchors us in that good space. That way, we don't get completely swept away by the tides of our own thoughts and emotions. It's easy to get swept away by changes. It's easy to see only the bad side of change, instead of the good side, as well.

Deep inside each one of us there is a living, silent, watchful space. That space is underneath all our thoughts and feelings. It's the space of awareness in which our thoughts and feelings appear.

It is like the center point of our lives. From there, we are aware of everything that happens to us. Wherever we go, it's still there. It's there when we fall asleep, and it's there when we wake up.

From there, we are aware of our own bodies, our own emotions, and our own thoughts. From this inner space, we are aware of everything that our senses tell us about the outside world. Mindfulness reminds us about this constant space.

Everything around that space is always changing. Our bodies change. Our emotions change, and our thoughts and beliefs change, too. All our circumstances change. But that space at the heart of us never changes.

Ask an old person how they feel deep inside, and they might tell you that they still feel like the same child they once were. Their bodies might have aches and pains now, and they may have wrinkles and gray hair, but deep inside they're just the same.

Practicing mindfulness helps us make our inner anchor strong enough and heavy enough to stabilize us on the ocean of life. Whatever happens, we can meet it with courage, heart, and love.

When our minds are clear and calm, we can read the compass needle of our own hearts. We can navigate towards what feels right. We can sail in the direction of what helps and heals. We can steer clear of anger, hate, fear, worry, and things that harm us, as well as things that harm other people. Mindfulness helps us see the difference more clearly.

Fill that silent space inside you with love, starting now. As you grow up, fill it with wisdom. Fill it with good feelings, and accept yourself from deep inside. Then, when difficult changes happen in life, you will always have a strong anchor. There will be one permanent thing in life that never changes. It's your center point, it's your best friend, and it's none other than the real you.

The last chapter is going to explore how to use mindfulness in practical ways in everyday life. Let's take a look.

11

PRACTICAL MINDFULNESS TO GUIDE A HAPPY LIFE

Live mindfully, and you will also live skillfully.

Someone who has mastered mindfulness is calmer, wiser, and has a heart full of appreciation. Their mind is clearer and their emotions are not as turbulent. Although difficult things still happen to a mindful person, they're able to handle troubles and setbacks with far more grace.

In this chapter, we are going to share some tips and tricks to make mindfulness a part of your everyday life. It can help in *any* situation, no matter how complicated. Over time, and with practice and repetition, it begins to feel completely natural and normal. Ultimately, being more mindful is just a great way to live.

For instance, there's power in **gratitude and appreciation**. When we focus our minds on what we appreciate, then our minds and hearts don't get so stuck on things that bother us. Make gratitude and appreciation a habit. Then, more and more often, you will start to notice what you *have* and what you *are*, rather than what you *don't have*. Here's one way to practice that.

Two Good Things

- Think of two good things in your life right now. Make this a daily habit, and do it often. You can add it to your mindful breathing exercise, your posture exercise, or wherever you like. Do it when you wake up, or do it before you go to bed.

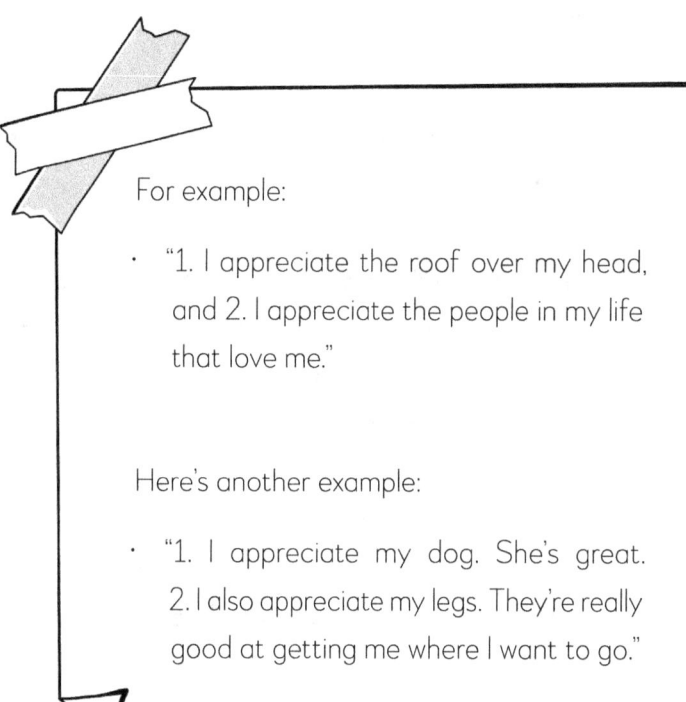

For example:

- "1. I appreciate the roof over my head, and 2. I appreciate the people in my life that love me."

Here's another example:

- "1. I appreciate my dog. She's great. 2. I also appreciate my legs. They're really good at getting me where I want to go."

- Take a moment to really feel that sense of appreciation. Choose two things you actually care about, and make it authentic. Hold that good, positive feeling inside you for a few mindful moments. Don't just let it slip away like any other thought.

Really try to find that true sense of appreciation. You might want to imagine you're baking that sense of gratitude and appreciation inside your mind and heart. Give it time to rise and set.

- Then, whenever things get difficult, just remember the two good things. It's never ALL bad.

Cultivating a sense of gratitude and appreciation is a good way to make friends with ourselves and deal with all the difficult parts of our lives. Even though we have challenges, they're usually wound up with the things we love and care about, too.

As one example, our friends are things we appreciate, but they're also people who can create some big challenges for us. As another example, our bodies are wonderful friends, but they can also be a nuisance sometimes. Good and bad tend to be wound up together.

That's especially true when it comes to relationships. Let's look at how mindfulness helps here, too.

Building Mindful Relationships

When we practice mindfulness, we learn how to get along with ourselves first. We accept the good and bad in us, and work with things the way they really are. When we can do that better, then getting along with other people becomes a little easier.

Nobody wants to go through life alone, and we all need friends. Sometimes, we worry that others won't like us or love us. That's often because there's something that we don't really like or love about ourselves. When we can accept ourselves just as we are and really love ourselves, then it's easier to accept other people just as they are. Acceptance builds trust, and that's a good way to start any relationship.

Here's a variation on the mindful heart exercise. It can help us to build better and more mindful relationships.

Heart Energy Connections

- Sit somewhere quietly, with a straight spine. Make sure you're not distracted.

- Breathe mindfully for a minute. Let go of the thoughts in your head. Stop chasing them and settle into your center.

- Put your hand on your heart. Feel your heartbeat. Feel the warmth in your body. Feel the life inside of you, even though you can't exactly explain it.

- Imagine that there's a stream of wonderful, bright energy in your heart area.

- As you breathe in, energy is flowing in, filling you up and making you feel good.

- Say to yourself, "I accept myself, just as I am today. I will be the best me that I can be."

- As you breathe out, energy is flowing out, and you're sharing your good feeling with the whole world around you. That beautiful energy connects to *everything*.

- Your stream of energy is so lovely that imaginary little creatures from all over are coming to drink from it. There are insects, birds, little animals, and people. When they taste the stream of energy, they feel refreshed and happy. That makes you happy, too. There's more than enough to go around. It just keeps bubbling up from somewhere.

- Think of someone you love and admire. Imagine that your stream of bright, refreshing love energy connects you to them. Feel it connecting, there in your heart.

- Now, imagine your heart area is like a giant dam of bright energy. Fill it up to the brim with good feelings.

- Take a few deep breaths, then come back. Go about your day with that feeling inside you, following you wherever you go. Whenever you talk to someone or look at someone, feel free to share that stream of good energy.

Talk Less, Listen More

Have you ever seen a deer in nature? Most of us have seen them on video, at least. They're so peaceful, and they have these amazing ears.

As they go about their deer day, doing their deer things, they're always alert. Their long, graceful ears swivel to catch every sound. Every once in a while, they look up while chewing peacefully, just to make sure. They're paying attention to every detail around them.

The deer is completely aware, *yet it isn't constantly stressed out*. It listens so totally that there's no room for mental chatter. If it hears a strange new sound, it will stop, standing like a statue. Its ears pick up the tiniest sound, and its sensitive nose twitches as it sniffs the air. It's ready for anything, completely present in the moment.

Mindfulness makes us receptive like that. Our mind becomes super-receptive, and we become more sensitive to thoughts and feelings, without stressing out. That helps us talk less and listen more.

Normally, our minds are like chatterboxes. We're always busy in our heads, thinking about what to say, what to do, and what's going on around us. When we speak to other people, we're often so busy thinking of what we want to say in reply that there's no space to listen. Before they finish their sentence, we're already coming up with a smart reply.

All that mental chatter can clutter up our relationships. Instead of really connecting to the other person, we're listening to our own thoughts in our heads. If we really pay attention and really listen to other people, things change.

Mindfulness helps us create space around our own thoughts and feelings. It also helps us create space around other people's thoughts and feelings. We allow room for them. We give those thoughts and feelings the respect, acceptance, and space they need to exist.

In mindful relationships, we're alert, like a deer's ears. We're never nervous or defensive. We also feel a greater sense of peace inside us, just like that beautiful, peaceful animal.

In that quiet, respectful space, as we're really paying attention to what someone else is saying, there's plenty of room for a good relationship.

The other person feels as if you're actually listening — as if you care. They sense that you're not judging them or trying to argue with them. You're accepting them as they are, and giving them the respect they are due. It's a great way to treat everybody, especially your friends and family.

If you're someone who struggles to talk less and listen more, you can take a lesson from nature.

- Imagine you're like that deer — completely peaceful, yet totally alert.

- Take one minute out of your day and really listen to the sounds around you. Try to catch as many as you can. Find the silences between each sound.

- Listen to the sound of your own breathing.

- As you go through your day, try to remind yourself of that peacefulness. Try to stay alert, yet peaceful.

- When someone talks to you, listen with great attention, instead of rushing to reply.

- Feel that peaceful silence underneath all the sounds in the outside world. It's there, underneath the noise of your own thoughts, too. Find that silence in between the different sounds.

Peace Talks: Handling Disagreements Without the Drama

You're a marvelous human being. You have the right to think what you think and feel what you feel. You have the right to express your thoughts and feelings, and it's completely natural to do so. Self-expression is an important part of life.

That doesn't mean you have to ignore the rest of the world, nor does it mean you're supposed to broadcast your thoughts and feelings all the time. Other people have the same rights and the same kinds of thoughts and feelings. Sometimes, it's just better to agree to disagree than to insist that your opinion is the only important one. Usually, silence is the best argument.

Our human minds love drama. There's a reason why movies and stories are so popular. Drama is a big part of all those movies and stories. Without disagreements, opposing thoughts and feelings, differences, and the occasional fight, the stories would be bland. Everyone would just get along and live happily ever after. That's great, but it's not much of a story.

Mindfulness helps us deal better with our drama. We don't have to treat disagreements as terribly important in life. We can survive quite easily without them — although they do make life more interesting. There's nothing wrong with a bit of drama or the occasional disagreement. The trick is not to take things so personally.

When we practice mindfulness, we're able to let go of thoughts and feelings more easily. We don't feel we have to fight to defend them so much. After all, they're just thoughts and feelings. They're just opinions. Maybe they're right, and maybe they're wrong.

Disagreements actually help us. They allow us to explore our thoughts and feelings with other people. They open our minds to new points of view. They allow us to see how other people think and feel. They make our world much bigger, richer, and more interesting.

Our disagreements become unpleasant when anger comes up. Differences of opinion become ugly when people feel the need to defend them at all costs. Arguments become difficult when we feel pressured and defensive. That happens when we feel personally threatened by what the other person says or believes.

Of course, if someone is really threatening to harm you, it's good to get out of the situation and ask for help. Nobody has the right to harm you. Usually, however, it's just an innocent disagreement gone wrong.

It's difficult to stay mindful during an argument or disagreement. The moment someone becomes angry, mindfulness has gone out the window. Try your best to stay present during such times, but if you fail, at least try to become mindful afterward.

How To Stay Mindful During An Argument

☆ Take a deep breath and let go. Take another deep breath, and, as you exhale slowly, let go even more. Release as much of the tension in your body as you can.

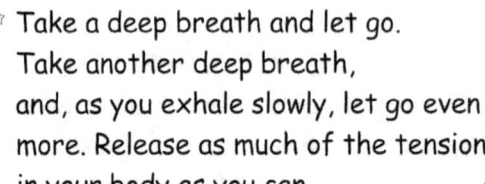

☆ Become mindful of the present moment. "I'm here. I'm present. I am aware of what's happening around me, and I'm aware of what's happening inside me — whether I like it or not."

☆ Remember that underneath the difficult thoughts and emotions is a peaceful space that is always there. You might not see it or feel it right now, but it's there. That's where you will return once this experience is over — and this experience won't last forever.

☆ If you feel angry or upset, start by noticing it and accepting it. "This is how I feel right now."

- Remind yourself that thoughts and feelings come and go.
  These thoughts and feelings won't be here forever, but you will still be here tomorrow, and so will the person with whom you had the disagreement.

- If you can make peace with that person right away, do so.

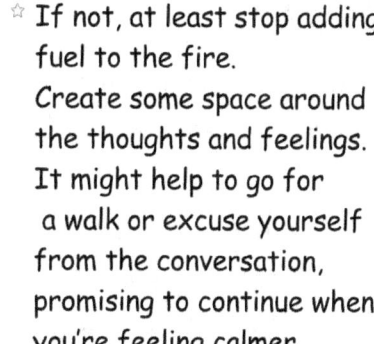

- If not, at least stop adding fuel to the fire.
  Create some space around the thoughts and feelings. It might help to go for a walk or excuse yourself from the conversation, promising to continue when you're feeling calmer.

- Allow the other person the freedom to feel what they feel, think whatever they think, and say what they say. That's their business. Disengage yourself from their angry energy.

As we've learned, mindfulness is about remembering and safeguarding a kind, peaceful space inside us. It creates room inside to breathe. That space helps us keep our balance in relationships.

When we make that happy place our inner home, it helps us to better accept our own thoughts and feelings. It also helps us accept and deal with the thoughts and feelings of other people. That's a nice bonus!

Letting Go

Very often, the things that bother us the most are the most difficult to let go of. It's a strange thing. Why do we cling to things that hurt us?

For example, George struggles to let go of grudges. If someone insults him, teases him, or acts in a way that he thinks is wrong, it's not easy for George to forgive and forget.

Two years ago, a boy in his class told George that he had a big nose. George didn't think he had a big nose, but that insult really bothered him. For a long time afterward, he felt self-conscious about his nose. Two years have passed, but every time George sees that boy, he remembers, and it still hurts. Inside of him, George is holding on tightly to that pain. He won't let go.

The other boy has completely forgotten about it. He actually admires George, in a way, because he's really good at soccer. But George doesn't know that. All he thinks about is that one day and that one insult. In George's mind, it's like a big mountain, whereas in reality, it's more like a little molehill. The problem is that all those grudges are making George unhappy a lot of the time. He knows it, but he still struggles to let go of his grudges.

Frieda struggles to let go of anxiety. Days before a big test, she winds herself up into a ball of tension. On the day of the test, she gets close to a panic attack. Even once the test has passed and Frieda has actually done quite well, she still feels anxious. She can't let go of that ball of tension in her body. It sits like a stone in her gut.

Frieda knows it's unhealthy and hurting her, but she can't let go. She really wants to do well at school and make her mother proud. It's important to her, so she keeps on doing the same thing. Every time there's a challenge, Frieda holds on to that feeling of anxiety. Maybe she believes that being anxious is somehow helping her do better at school — but deep down, she actually knows better.

Why do we keep holding on to things that harm us? Usually, it's because we're not completely mindful of what we're doing.

Mindfulness can help us let go of difficult thoughts and feelings that are hurting us. When we bring our thoughts and feelings out into the light, we can work with them in an honest way. We can't do that if we ignore them, pretend they're not there, or bury them.

We can't ignore our feelings and thoughts. It's useless to sweep them under the rug, because doing so will only cause more trouble.

Looking inward in a mindful way can bring those thoughts and feelings to the surface. We become aware of them and we can face them head-on. Then we can examine them in a kind, accepting way. After that, we can try to do what we can to improve matters and let go of the rest.

But that's the big question though: How do we let go?

First, become aware of what you need to let go of. Identify it clearly. Next, accept that things are the way they are. Think carefully about whether there is still something you can do to improve matters. Can you fix things? Can you forgive someone? Is there something constructive you can do to help? When you've done all you can, it's no longer in your control. Accept that it's time to let it be, then move on.

Letting go isn't just the thought "I let go." It has to feel real. It has to come from deep inside, and it must include your emotions and your body.

Here's a way to practice letting go. It's a favorite with many young people. If you're struggling to move on from a difficult experience, have a thought that keeps recurring, or have an emotion you want to release, this might help.

Thought Bubbles

- Get comfortable in a quiet place and enter your mindful zone. Take a few deep breaths and then settle into your center.

- Focus only on your breathing for a while, until you begin to relax more deeply.

- Now, identify the thought, emotion, or experience you want to release.

- Imagine that you're putting it into a bubble of light.

- Feel the feeling, and put that into the bubble. Think about it, name it, or write it on an imaginary note and put it in there. If there's somewhere in your body that feels tight or constricted by that thought and feeling, send that into the bubble, as well, using your imagination.

- Say to your bubble, "Thank you for visiting me, but it's time to go. I've learned a lot from you, but I don't need you anymore. Goodbye bubble."

- Let go.

- Let go of the thought, completely.

- Let go of the emotion. Let it be what it is. Let it out. If you want to cry, then cry. If you want to holler, then holler. Let it out.

- Let go of the feeling in your body that is stuck and holding on tight. Relax it completely and let go.

- Watch that bubble float up into the sky. See it move off.

- Watch it become smaller and smaller, until you can't see it anymore.

- Come back into your center. Breathe. You're okay.

The thought or feeling may try to come back and bother you some more. That's not necessarily a failure. Some things are stuck so deep inside us that it takes a while to get free.

You may want to repeat the bubble exercise again. It might help to talk things through with someone you trust. It might help to run, punch a punching bag, or go on a journey into nature and let go in peace. Do what you need to do, but let go and move on. Keep on letting go until it doesn't return.

Whatever the thought, emotion, or experience is, you're bigger and stronger than it. If you let go of it, it will let go of you, too.

Find that empty, peaceful space inside you. Don't clutter it with harmful thoughts and feelings. When they start taking up too much space, become mindful and clear out the room.

Creating a Mindful Environment at Home and School

Mindfulness creates an eco-friendly environment inside our minds and hearts. In other words, it's healthy, balanced, and alive. A mindful person is vibrant, flowing, and natural, like a beautiful piece of nature.

As we become clear inside — as we become skilled at staying mindful — the world around us is affected in a positive way, too. To help with that, it might be useful to add mindful elements to your home and school environment wherever you can.

Here are some things you might want to experiment with:

- **Remind yourself to stay friends with your own mind.** You might want to put up a note somewhere, or a funny picture that reminds you. Making friends with your mind will help you learn better and keep a balance in your thinking. Make a poster, get an ornament that looks like a brain, or just write out the sentence "My mind is my good friend."

- **Be mindful of technology.** Take note of how much time you spend on your phone or in front of a screen. If you love that kind of thing — and so many of us do — why not add a mindfulness app or documentary into the mix? There's nothing wrong with screens, but they do have a way of making us less present in the moment.

    While you're scrolling, browsing, or watching, take regular breaks. Come back into your own skin. Look outside, or, even better, go outside for a while. Get some sunlight, look at the horizon, and remind yourself that you're a real, live human being. Stay tech-mindful.

- **Create a mindfulness space**. It's easy to get distracted when practicing mindfulness, especially at the beginning. Make it easier on yourself by creating your own mindful zone. Get some comfortable cushions, or make a special corner somewhere. Put some things there that help you feel comfortable, mindful, and peaceful, or make it as empty as a Zen dojo — whatever works for you. Make it personal, clutter-free, screen-free, and special. Go there regularly to practice mindfulness. You may want to add other spaces, such as a little corner somewhere at school, or in a park that you often go to.

- **Practice any time.** Nobody has to know that you're practicing mindfulness. You might be sitting on a bus or working quietly in class. You might be sitting in the back seat of a car or walking home from school. Use those in-between moments to practice. You don't always have to sit still with a straight spine. At any moment, you can become deeply aware of the present. You can turn your torch light of awareness inwards and watch your own thoughts and feelings. You can sense your whole body any time you like, and nobody needs to know that you're looking inwards. Just come into the here and now and be deeply mindful.

- **Team mindfulness**. At its most basic essence, mindfulness is a solo thing. It's something you discover and explore within yourself. Even so, it helps to have a team. Other people can remind you and encourage you to keep developing your mindful skills. If your parents understand the benefits of mindfulness, they may be great members of team mindfulness. Find like-minded people and create a mindful support group to help you grow your peace and inner joy. Mindfulness is not a big secret anymore. It's not like during the time of Zen, or like ancient India! There are plenty of people in the world who would like to be more mindful, too.

I hope that these suggestions will encourage you to keep exploring and developing your mindfulness. Our journey together is coming to an end, so it's time to summarize it all and leave you with one final positive message.

CONCLUSION

A mindful young person is a wise young person who lives skillfully. Throughout this book, we've explored what that means and how to do it.

Being mindful is actually quite simple to understand, but it's not that easy to do in real life. It means being able to rise above our own thoughts and emotions, as well as the thoughts and emotions of other people.

That skill gives us great power. It lets us handle difficult situations with a lot more grace. It helps us experience less stress and navigate change far more smoothly. It can help us rid ourselves of negative thought habits and ride out strong emotional currents.

It's not exactly a brand-new idea. People have known about mindfulness for a very long time. It may have appeared in different places with different names, but the basic idea is intuitive. Any thinking person can appreciate what it means, as long as they take the time to investigate the wave patterns of their own thoughts and feelings.

Our minds and our brains coexist. They go together. Our emotions and our bodies are joined to each other, and they're linked to our minds, too. Mindfulness helps us bring harmony to these different parts of being human. Body, mind, and feelings start to cooperate, as if they're dancing to the same music.

To master the art of mindfulness, we need two things. First, we need to understand why it works, and test it in real life to see if it's really true. Once we're personally convinced that it works, it will naturally motivate us to keep practicing.

That's the second thing we need — practice. Even though we understand how it works, mindfulness won't be effective until it becomes a habit in our minds, feelings, and bodies. Mindfulness needs to become like a well-trodden pathway in life. Otherwise, it will fade.

Remember Jenny, the surfer girl? She had to fall off her board many times before she learned how to keep her balance. In the end, it was worth it, because surfing is the best feeling in the world for her. Practice makes perfect.

I hope that this book inspires you to really get to know your own mind, your own feelings and your deepest sense of self. May it help you live a skillful and awesome life as you grow into an adult. You may find that this skill is a keeper for life. No matter what our age, mindfulness is a great asset to have.

Stay mindful, and stay happy.

THANKS
FOR READING MY
BOOK!

I appreciate you picking this guide to empower your tweens with the skills they need to understand and manage their emotions confidently.

I would be so grateful if you could take a moment to leave an honest review or a star rating on Amazon.
(A star rating is just a couple of clicks away.)

By leaving a review, you'll help other parents discover this valuable resource for their own children. Thank you!

To leave a review & help spread the word

www.ingramcontent.com/pod-product-compliance
Lightning Source LLC
Chambersburg PA
CBHW072054110526
44590CB00018B/3173